MONEY TALKS

One of the consequences of Britain's economic ills.
26 January 1982. (John Topham)

Edited by
ALAN HORROX and GILLIAN McCREDIE

MONEY TALKS

Five views
of Britain's economy
by
MILTON FRIEDMAN
MAURICE PESTON
SAM AARONOVITCH
AJIT SINGH
IRENE BRUEGEL

Thames Methuen · London 1983

Money Talks features essays by those who contributed to the Thames Television series of the same name.
Television production by: Jill Fullerton-Smith, Alan Horrox, Peter Lock, Gillian McCredie.

First published in Great Britain 1983
by Thames Television International Ltd
149 Tottenham Court Road, London W1P 9LL

Distributed by Methuen (Associated Book Publishers)
11 New Fetter Lane, London EC4P 4EE

Copyright © 1983 by the contributors and Thames Television

All rights reserved. No part of this publication shall be reproduced, stored in a retrieval system, or transmitted, in any form or by any means, electronic, mechanical, photocopying, recording or otherwise, without the prior permission of the copyright owners.

ISBN 0 423 00790 4

Cover design and photograph by Trevor Key
Book design by Thames Television Publishing Department
Phototypeset by Shanta Thawani, London N11
Printed in Great Britain by Whitstable Litho, Whitstable, Kent

Contents

Some Thoughts on Money	vi
Introduction	vii
A Monetarist View MILTON FRIEDMAN	1
A Keynesian View MAURICE PESTON	18
A Marxist View SAM AARONOVITCH	34
A Third World View AJIT SINGH	54
A Feminist View IRENE BRUEGEL	75

Figures

1	Money and prices, 1964-81, in Britain	8
2	Money and prices, 1964-81, in Japan	8
3	Money and prices, 1964-81, in United States	8
4	Money and prices, 1964-81, in Brazil	8
5	Money supply and prices, 1971-8, in Japan	12
6	Britain's monetary growth (M1) 1964-80	13
7	Unemployment in Britain, 1979-82	28
8	Inflation in Britain, 1978-82	28
9	World unemployment, 1979-82	56
10	Manufacturing jobs in Britain, 1968-78	56
11	Decline in manufacturing output in depression of 1870s, 1930s, 1980s.	57
12	Relative income per head, in India and Britain, 1800 and 1982.	63
13	Car production in Japan and United States, 1950s and 1970s.	66
14	British trade balance with NICs and other trading partners.	70

Money is like a sixth sense without which you cannot make a complete use of the other five.
— W. SOMERSET MAUGHAM

I've never known an emotion that cannot satisfactorily be expressed by money. — CLARENCE DARROW

With money in your pocket, you are wise and you are handsome, and you sing well too. — YIDDISH PROVERB

When money speaks, the truth keeps silent.
— RUSSIAN PROVERB

If you would know what the Lord God thinks of money, you have only to look at those to whom he gives it.
— MAURICE BARING

The love of money is the root of all evil. — THE BIBLE

Go into the street, and give one man a lecture on morality, and another a shilling, and see which will respect you most. — SAMUEL JOHNSON

Money can't buy friends, but you can get a better class of enemy. — SPIKE MILLIGAN

There was a time when a fool and his money were soon parted, but now it happens to everybody.
— ADLAI STEVENSON

One must choose, in life, between making money and spending it. There's no time to do both.
— EDOUARD BOURDET

Anyone who lives within his means suffers from a lack of imagination. — LIONEL STANDER

A penny saved is a penny to squander.
— AMBROSE BIERCE

Introduction

'Money is paper blood,' said Bob Hope. Each one of us puzzles, dreams, worries about money for much of our lives. For most people, its importance rivals every other source of human pleasure and pain. But what is money? Its existence is mythical, founded on an arbitrary social convention which attaches value to slips of paper with pictures of the Queen on them, just as our ancestors attached value to weapons, shells, tea, tobacco and even lumps of stone. For them, money was not so much functional as magical, and over the centuries money has lost none of this magic. Those magical and meaningless words 'I promise to pay the bearer...' sanctify our modern system of financial exchange upon which industrial society is founded. Over the years money has become one way, perhaps the only way, of assessing and possessing 'value'. It stands at the hub of every form of human exchange, more important, arguably, than speech itself. But although most of us may be obsessed with money, few people know or care a great deal about the study of money – economics.

Economics seems baffling, intimidating, boring. This might not matter if Britain were not currently facing severe economic problems, with among the lowest growth and highest unemployment of all industrial countries. For this reason, Thames Television invited five leading economists to sum up, in a single essay, their diagnosis of Britain's ills and their prescription for the cure.

In the first essay, Milton Friedman explains monetarism, the economic viewpoint of Mrs Thatcher's government. He argues that Britain's problems of inflation and slow growth can only be solved by a combination of monetary controls, less government and more free enterprise.

Maurice Peston then explains the Keynesian approach applied by most post-war British governments until the election of Mrs Thatcher. He turns on its head the popular belief that 'we cannot spend more than we earn,' and argues for urgent government action to stimulate public demand and create more jobs.

Sam Aaronovitch explores, from a Marxist viewpoint, the historical reasons for Britain's decline, as successive governments protected our international role at the expense of our national industries. He argues that only a shift towards democratic control of industry can reverse this decline.

Ajit Singh then outlines the dramatic changes in the world economy since World War II. He charts the astounding growth of the newly industrialized countries (NICs for short) like Mexico, Brazil, Singapore and Taiwan, and predicts that before long any or all of these newcomers may become the Japan of tomorrow, facing the older industrial countries with even fiercer competition.

In the last essay, Irene Bruegel examines an area ignored by most male economists – the unpaid work of women in the home, which services the male workforce and produces workers for the future. She argues that only a radical redistribution of both paid and unpaid work would offer women greater freedom and would also help solve Britain's unemployment.

Each of these five essays offers a very different account of how the economy works and what can be done to make it work better. They offer a challenge to readers to decide for themselves which account, if any, makes most sense of the workings of that strange commodity, money.

ALAN HORROX

MILTON FRIEDMAN

A Monetarist View

The discussion of economic policy in Great Britain is bedevilled by two major confusions. One is the confusion between science and ideology. The other is the confusion about the meaning of monetarism.

Economics is a science which has something to say about the way the world works. Its purpose is to try to tell you; if you do this, this will happen. As a science it has nothing to say about what you *should* do. That depends on your ideology. That depends on your values, on your beliefs, on what it is you want to accomplish.

The other confusion, which is equally serious, is about the meaning of monetarism. In Great Britain, monetarism has come to cover a very wide range of subjects. Indeed, it has come to be identified with whatever it is that Prime Minister Margaret Thatcher proposed when she first came into office in 1979. That is understandable, but confusing, because monetarism in fact deals with only one part of Margaret Thatcher's programme - that part of her programme which had to do with controlling inflation by restraining the growth in the quantity of money.

I happen to agree with almost the whole of Margaret Thatcher's programme, but that is not because of my monetarist views as a scientific economist; it is because I share her conception of what is necessary for Britain to become healthy. It is perfectly possible for people to agree about scientific propositions and not to agree about policy. For example, believe it or not, Karl Marx, Communist China and I all accept the scientific analysis of monetarism - the 'quantity' theory of money. But you can be sure we do not agree about much else.

Left: Karl Marx: an early monetarist? 'It is perfectly possible for people to agree about scientific propostions and not to agree about policy.' In the sense that he accepted the scientific theory, Marx was a monetarist. (BBC Hulton Picture Library). *Right:* Adam Smith, British economist, published *The Wealth of Nations* in 1776, a major work of political economy. The 'quantity' theory of money features in economic thought even this early. (BBC Hulton Picture Library)

What is monetarism?

Let me turn to what monetarism is really about. It deals with one narrow but very important subject: the relationship between quantity of money on the one hand and, on the other, such economic variables as total income in pounds (or other units), the level of prices, economic fluctuations, and interest rates.

It has nothing to say about such other subjects as whether the government budget should be large or small, or whether taxes should be raised or lowered. Those are very important subjects, but they are dealt with in other branches of economics, not in monetarism. Monetarism has become a sort of code word, but in fact it is simply a new name for a very ancient doctrine, the 'quantity' theory of money. The study of this goes back for centuries. There is a long literature, much of it derived from British economists, dealing

A Monetarist View

with the quantity theory of money. John Maynard Keynes, who is regarded as the very opposite of monetarist, made very important contributions to the quantity theory of money. For much of his career, he was a monetarist.

The key element in the monetarist view is the distinction between the *nominal* quantity of money - the amount of money in a country expressed in terms of pounds or dollars or francs - and the *real* quantity of money - not the pieces of paper, but what those pieces of paper will buy. The nominal quantity of money may double, and yet the total volume of goods and services which it buys may not change.

The key proposition in monetarism is that the monetary authorities - in Great Britain, the Bank of England; in the United States, the Federal Reserve System - can control the *nominal* amount of money expressed in pounds or in dollars, but cannot control the real quantity of money. It is the public at large, the consumers, the holders of money, who decide what the real quantity of money will be. This is a very difficult concept for the non-economist to grasp. The reason it is so difficult is that what is true for the country as a whole is the opposite of what is true for each individual separately.

This is a very common feature. Imagine a crowded theatre. If one person wanted to get out of that theatre, he or she would be able to get out in a minute or two. But suppose somebody cried 'fire' and everybody tried to get out of the theatre all at once; it would be a very different situation. The same holds in the monetary area. To each person separately it appears that, given the total amount of his wealth, he can decide what fraction of it he would like to keep as a reserve in the form of currency in his pocket, or in deposits readily available in the bank. And indeed, if someone decided that for whatever reason he wanted to have some more currency in his pocket, he could go to the bank and get it.

For the country as a whole, however, the total amount of money to be held is fixed. The Bank of England has seen to that. There is a total amount of currency, plus an

Monetary authorities control the *nominal* amount of money, but cannot control the *real* value.
Top: the Federal Reserve Bank, Washington.
Bottom: the Bank of England in the City of London.

A Monetarist View

amount of deposits available. One person can get more only by bidding it away from someone else. More for one means less for the other.

Another reason why there is so much confusion about monetary relations is that changes in the quantity of money, though extremely important, do not have instantaneous and precise effects. If, at the very moment when the quantity of money changed, people could see that everything else changed, they would not be confused about what was going on. But that is not the way it works. It takes a long time for changes in the quantity of money to work their way through the system, and they work their way differently at different times.

Cheap money makes dear goods
Suppose the quantity of money starts rising more rapidly – because the Bank of England has decided that the country ought to have an infusion of more money, or because it has made a miscalculation, or for whatever reason. In olden times it might have been because somebody discovered gold, but this could not be so today; today it is the government that determines the quantity of money.

If the quantity of money starts rising more rapidly, people will discover that they have a little more cash in their pockets. Now they may not want to have any more cash around. Perhaps they need enough cash to be able to cover their spending for a week, but now they have enough for ten days. Well then, they will try to convert that extra cash into other goods, by spending it – maybe by buying on the stock exchange, or perhaps by going to the stores.

There are all sorts of ways the cash might be spent. But however it is done, the first effect will be that total spending will go up; that in turn will come to the dealers, retailers and wholesalers, as an increase in demand. They will not know whether that is going to last or be temporary, so at first they will meet it by producing more goods or selling more goods, taking it out of stocks. But the impact will be temporary, because if the increase in the quantity of money continues, the spending will keep on going up and, after a point, the retailers will recognise what is going on and will start marking up prices to contain demand.

Again, remember the difference between what is true for an individual and what is true for society. If you decide that you want to buy more shoes, you can go out and buy them and that is not going to raise the price of shoes. But if everybody in the country is trying to buy more shoes, that will surely raise the price of shoes.

On average, an increase in the quantity of money takes something like six months before it starts to affect output. Although, to begin with, a change in the quantity of money will affect output and employment, in the long run its major effect will be on prices. That is why inflation is always and everywhere a monetary phenomenon.

Inflation has one cause
Some people say the reason why prices go up is that wages go up: it is the bad labour unions that drive up wages. Others say the reason prices go up is that greedy businessmen are trying to increase their profits, by raising their prices. Or perhaps it is because of those terrible consumers who rush out and buy goods and services, and that too drives prices up.

That is all utter nonsense. People who work always want higher wages; businessmen always want higher profits; consumers are always spendthrifts. But we have not always had inflation. Sometimes prices have come down.

The fact is that inflation is always and everywhere a monetary phenomenon. There has never been an inflation in the course of history, which has not been produced by an excessively rapid rate of increase in the quantity of money. The quantity of money has come up faster than total output and the result inevitably has been a rise in prices.

Governments have tried to interfere by price and wage control. It has never worked. The Roman Emperor Diocletian, two thousand years ago, tried to

A Monetarist View

prevent inflation by very rigid control over prices and wages. It broke down then. It has been tried repeatedly over two thousand years since. It has broken down every time. We have had that experience in Britain

Coins of the Roman Emperor Diocletian (245-313), an early exponent of price and wage controls. (British Museum)

repeatedly. The most that can be done by this is to postpone the evil day and then when it comes it is even worse.

Inflation is caused by one thing only - more rapid increase in the quantity of money than in output. I could go on explaining this at great length, but I think I can show it more effectively with the aid of charts.

Figure 1 shows what happened to the quantity of money in Great Britain, relative to output, over the past twenty years. As you can see, it went up pretty steadily during the period. It also shows what happened to the level of prices during the period. If the lines were not labelled, it would be hard to tell which was which. They move together, not by accident, but because it is the increase in the quantity of money that has produced the increase in the level of prices. In Figures 2 and 3, for Japan and the US, the two variables also move together.

Figure 4 showing the situation of Brazil, illustrates the relationship in a very extreme manner. In Brazil they have had a really whopping inflation. The inflation rate sometimes reached one hundred per cent per year. As the chart shows, the relationship is the

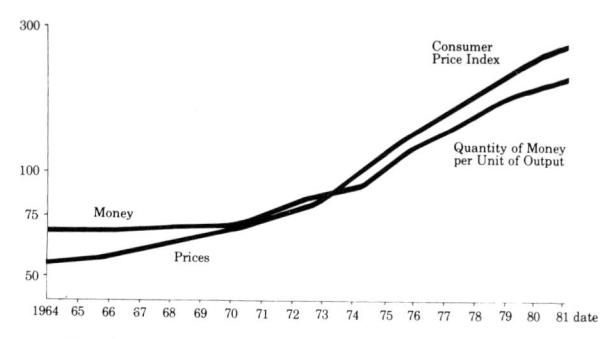

Figure 1. Graph showing the movement of Consumer Price Index and Quantity of Money per Unit of Output for Great Britain, 1964-81. The vertical scale is logarithmic.

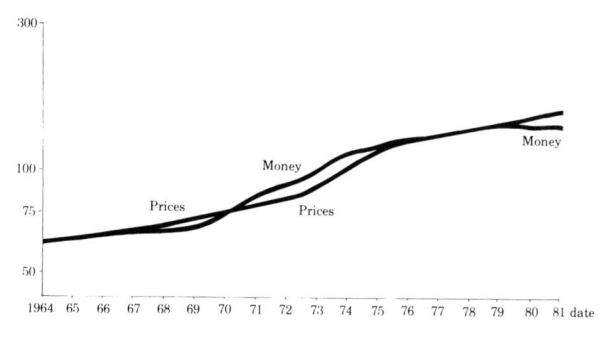

Figure 2. Japan.

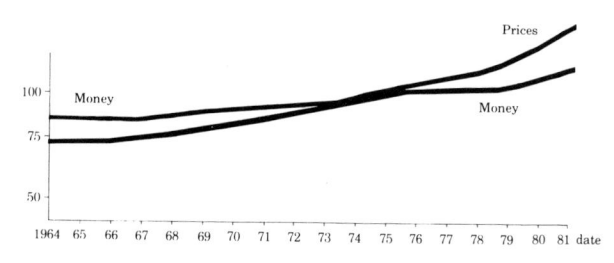

Figure 3. United States.

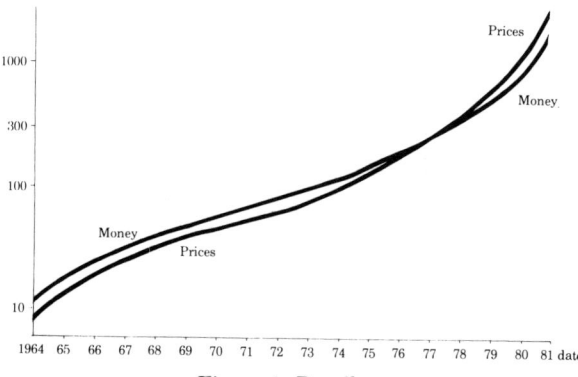

Figure 4. Brazil.

A Monetarist View

same; the two curves are almost indistinguishable from one another.

Which comes first: the increase in money or the increase in prices? Some people say the fact that the two move together does not prove which causes which. There is considerable evidence to show that the changes in money are always first. They *precede* the changes in prices and produce the changes in prices. In societies of very different economic arrangements and very different banking systems, the same phenomenon has been observed.

What is to be done?

Let me turn now to problems of policy. So far my analysis has been purely scientific. If a government wants to produce inflation, then this analysis will tell it how to do it. If a government wants to produce deflation, this analysis will tell it how to do it. It is neutral with respect to policy. But I now want to turn and discuss the issues of policy that are common to the United States and Great Britain.

Speaking broadly, there are two major problems that we have been facing. One has been the problem of inflation; the other has been the problem of relatively slow growth, and particularly the difficulties both countries have had in trying to curtail the rate of inflation.

These two problems of inflation and slow growth are related to one another in Britain and the United States, but they are fundamentally independent. It would be possible, in a society, to have no inflation and no growth. Portugal under Salazar was a very good example. It would be possible for a society to have high inflation and high growth. Israel in an earlier period was an example.

But in the modern world, in Britain and the United States, those are not possibilities. Inflation will, sooner or later, in countries in their circumstances, lead to slow growth. That is why that miserable, unpleasant word stagflation was coined to describe the combination of inflation and stagnation.

The way in which slow growth and inflation are related is that both of them reflect the excessive growth of government. Government spending has grown. It has grown, not because the people who run government are bad people, but because you and I and all the rest of the citizens have asked governments to do things and have all thought that somebody else was going to pay for it.

The problem that we have all faced was described very well by the French economist Frederick Bastiat, a century and a half ago, when he said 'government is that fiction whereby everybody believes he can live at the expense of everybody else.'

Government spending has grown, and it has grown beyond the point at which citizens are really willing to pay openly, explicitly, enough taxes to finance that spending. So governments have naturally tried to find some way to spend without imposing taxes.

It cannot be done. The total tax imposed on the people is what government spends, and that is the amount of money the people do not have the power to spend. But there is one form of taxation that can be imposed without anybody voting for it, and that is inflation. Let the government finance its expenditure by printing money, and it will be able to spend. It *looks* as if it is not imposing taxes, but the result is inflation, which is a hidden tax, and in many ways the most destructive tax of all.

It is the rapid expansion of government which is also responsible for slowing of growth, for the failure of our countries to achieve the kind of progress we should be able to make. Government has absorbed more and more of the total income of the people in Britain and now it is something over half. Each citizen in Britain works from 1st January to some time in July to pay the expenses of government; only after that can he or she work for himself or herself. Is he getting his money's worth? The citizens of Britain can answer that question better than I. But nobody spends somebody else's money as well, as carefully, and as economically as he spends his own. That is why the growth of government

A Monetarist View

has meant less effective use of resources. In addition, government has imposed rules and regulations, intervened here and there, nationalised industries and levied high taxes which have reduced people's incentives to work, to save, to invest. The combination of all has resulted in slow growth. That is why inflation and slow growth are so very closely related.

I come to the question of how you cure these problems. What are the cures for inflation on the one hand and for slow growth on the other? The cure for inflation is very easy to state, but very hard to bear. There is one and only one cure for inflation: to reduce the rate of monetary growth. There is no other cure; no nation has ever cured inflation in any other way. But that cure is hard to take, because the most effective way to reduce the rate of monetary growth is to cut down government spending. People do not like that. In addition, in the early stages, the effects of cutting down inflation are not very pleasant; it tends to create unemployment and to produce a recession. Do not suppose there is a painless way to end inflation; there is no magic pill that will solve our ills without discomfort. But the alternative is more painful still. Britain's experience over the past several decades shows that as inflation rises, unemployment rises too.

Once a nation embarks on inflation, it has no good alternative. If it keeps on inflating, it will get higher unemployment. If it cures inflation, it will temporarily have higher unemployment. If it goes to a still higher level of inflation, it may for a time be able, artificially, to speed up the economy, but only at the cost of creating a problem later, of a still more serious nature.

The funny thing about inflation as produced by the increase in the quantity of money, is that it is like drinking. The good effects come first and the bad effects come much later. That is why people are tempted to drink too much, and why countries are tempted to inflate too much. But the problem can be overcome. Consider the case of Japan, the most successful example of a cure for inflation that I know of.

Figure 5 shows that in 1973 the quantity of money

was growing at more than twenty-five per cent each year. At the same time inflation was starting to rise very, very rapidly. The Japanese saw what was coming and decided to do something about it. In 1973 they started to cut down the rate of monetary growth very drastically, bringing it down to between ten and fifteen per cent.

For a time inflation continued to rise, until it too hit about twenty-five per cent each year. During the period

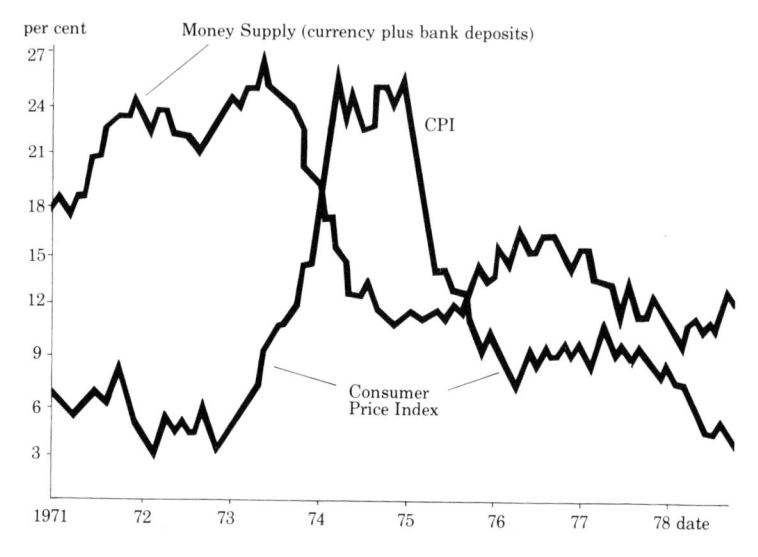

Figure 5. Graph showing movement in Japan, of Money Supply (currency plus bank deposits) and Consumer Price Index, as percentage increase from same month a year earlier.

when the quantity of money was coming down and inflation was still rising, Japan was having a very difficult time. It went through what, for Japan, was a very severe recession. But that only lasted for less than a year and a half, and then, as the quantity of money kept coming down, so did inflation. Inflation started down, and economic growth started up. The Japanese started to have an improvement in their economic condition and a more rapid growth in income. For the next four or five years, inflation kept coming down,

A Monetarist View

until by 1978 it was below five per cent; and yet, at the same time, economic activity continued to be very good. That is, I think, about the most successful example I know of a straightforward monetarist cure for inflation by a policy of slow and relatively steady monetary growth.

Has monetarism worked in Great Britain?

In one sense monetarism has succeeded in Britain, in another it has not. The aim of Margaret Thatcher when she came in, was to slow the rate of monetary growth in

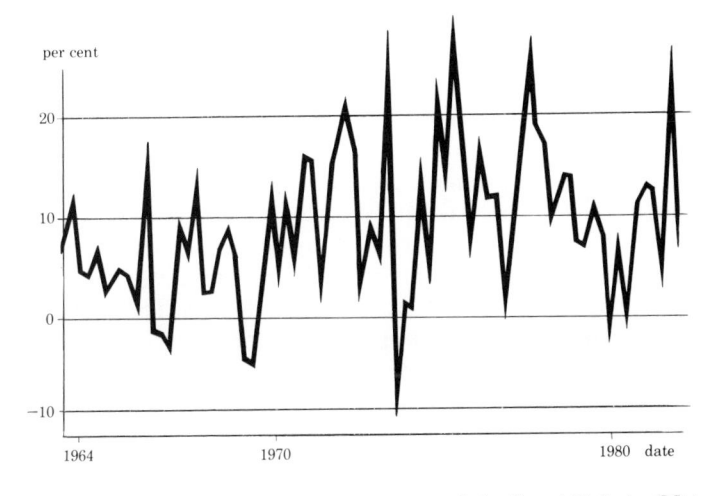

Figure 6. Graph showing monetary growth in Great Britain (M1), 1964-80. Annual rate of change, per cent, plotted quarterly.

order to cure inflation. Monetary growth has slowed. It has been cut down, and inflation has come down quite sharply. In that sense monetarism has worked and done everything that was promised for it. On the other hand, it is an essential ingredient of monetary policy that monetary growth not only be slow but also be *steady*. This has not been so in Britain.

Changes in the quantity of money which are erratic mean that the economy will be subject to a great deal of uncertainty and will have a very erratic pattern of behaviour. That is why those of us who are called

Margaret Thatcher. A convinced monetarist.

monetarists have always believed that it is very desirable to have a steady rate of monetary growth, and not to have it highly erratic.

In that sense monetarism has not worked because it has not been carried out. Figure 6 shows what has been happening, from quarter to quarter, to the rate of monetary growth in Britain. It shows a very erratic pattern, with sharp ups and sharp downs. The last few years in that chart represent the period when, supposedly, monetarism was being applied. It is very hard to see a much steadier rate of growth during that period than earlier. It is most unfortunate that monetary growth in Britain has been so erratic. In my opinion that has made the cost of shifting from a high inflation to a low inflation much greater in Britain than it need have been. It was not necessary to have gone through as serious a recession as Britain has gone through in order to bring inflation down. One of the reasons why the recession has been so serious is because of the unsteadiness of monetary growth.

That is not the only reason. The other reason, equally important, is because Margaret Thatcher's government has not succeeded in cutting sharply the size of government. Total government spending has not been brought down, and as a result too large a fraction of the resources of the country are still being employed in government. I am an admirer of Margaret Thatcher; I

A Monetarist View

do not attribute the failure in this respect to *her*. It is due rather to opposition from members within her own party and to opposition from the civil service, which obviously doesn not like to see its size cut down.

As for the cure for slow growth, the important problem, once again, is to cut down the size of government, to see that citizens no longer have to work from January to July or later to pay for the expenses of government, but can instead have greater control over their own lives. As I said, nobody spends somebody else's money as carefully as he spends his own.

Government enterprise is not efficient. Inflation has come down much more sharply in the private sector than it has come down in the government sector. The only cure for slow growth in Great Britain, as in the USA, is to allow the market to have a greater role, to cut down the extent to which it is controlled from the centre; to increase the extent to which private individuals can pursue their own objectives in their own way; and to give full scope for the ability, the enterprise, the initiative of British citizens. In my opinion there is nothing wrong with Britain that a dose of less government would not cure.

The economic foundation of freedom

Allow me to conclude by making a statement outside of science and on the level of ideology. I am an economist, but I am also a human being and a citizen of the US and someone who is very greatly interested in what happens in Great Britain. My basic value is a belief in human freedom.

I want a world in which people are free to pursue their own values, to say what they want, so long as they do not interfere with the freedom of others to do the same thing. Why is it so important from that perspective to cure inflation and to reduce the size of government? The reason is that inflation is an insidious disease which, if it is not checked, will destroy the whole fabric of the society. I do not know anybody who has put this better than the great British economist John Maynard Keynes, who wrote back in the twenties:

'Economic freedom is a necessary condition for political freedom.' One kind of economic freedom is the freedom to invest, through stocks. This is the floor of the new London Stock Exchange.

'There is no subtler, no surer means of overturning the existing basis of society than to debauch the currency. The process engages all the hidden forces of economic law on the side of destruction and does it in a manner which not one man in a million is able to diagnose.'

That is the reason why it is so important to cure inflation. But why is it important to cut the size of government? To get taxes lower, to enable people to keep a larger fraction of their income, so they do not have to keep working from January to July (or later) to pay the expenses of government; above all because you cannot have and retain political freedom unless you retain a large measure of economic freedom.

Economic freedom is not enough to assure political freedom. There have been many countries that have enjoyed a large measure of economic freedom but which have not had political freedom. But economic freedom is a necessary condition for political freedom.

A Monetarist View

In all of human history I know of no example of a country with a large degree of political freedom which has not relied in the main on private markets and private arrangements for organising its economic activity. That is why it is so important that we restrain government and cut it down to size. If we do not do so, then the marvellous heritage that Britain and America have had, of a free society, of personal liberty, will be destroyed.

MAURICE PESTON

A Keynesian View

The British economy is made up of two parts – a private sector and a public sector. About seventy per cent of us work in the private sector producing most of the goods and services that we buy, from washing machines to loaves of bread. But some thirty per cent of us work in the public sector (i.e. in government-owned industry or the government itself). This too produces some of the things we buy such as gas or electricity or public transport. But it also gives us a health service and education, old age pensions and payments to the needy.

Today, however, there is another sizeable sector to take notice of. About one in seven of us, while we are available for work, and in most cases have held jobs, are unemployed. Although we live in a system in which it is usual for adults to work in order to support themselves, the mixed economy is unable to provide jobs for over three million of them. For over a decade now, the British economy has not operated at full employment. For the previous twenty-five years, there was full employment. The economy grew faster than it had ever done before, and we were richer than we had ever been. One reason for this was that the ideas of John Maynard Keynes were generally accepted, and government policy based on them.

What Keynes taught
Keynesianism is a general system of economics, and gives rise to policy recommendations to deal with all sorts of problems. It was devised initially to explain unemployment and to offer remedies to get rid of it.

Keynes himself, despite his Eton and Cambridge background, was devoted to the study of the causes of unemployment with a view to devising policy measures

John Maynard Keynes (1883-1946) developed a system of economics which helps to analyse unemployment, and can provide policy guidelines for what to do about it. (BBC Hulton Picture Library).

Unemployment in the 1930s. Avoidable? (Museum of Labour History)

to get rid of it. He was much affected by the rise in unemployment in the slump of the early 1930s. The number of jobless then was similar to what it is today, but it then represented a much larger share of the labour force. The problem was also more significant because incomes then were lower. Poor workers had little by way of savings to fall back on, and unemployment pay was not high, nor was it so widely available.

Keynes and his colleagues differed from many economists and politicians not so much because they deplored unemployment but because they argued that practical steps could be taken to get rid of it. That remains the central message of Keynesianism today. Keynes would not have sat back and said, 'We can do nothing about the present scale of unemployment'. If he had been confronted with the prediction that the number of people out of work would go on rising, and could still be some three to four million by 1990, he would have been horrified. He would have pressed, on Churchillian lines, for 'action this day'. Indeed, although there are many basic differences between Keynesianism and such fashionable doctrines as monetarism, the key one is the emphasis placed by Keynes and his followers on the necessity and the feasibility of active economic policy.

Curiously enough, there is an association in the public mind between Keynesianism and left wing ideas and polices. But Keynes was never a socialist, and he showed little sympathy with socialism in any form. He was a liberal, and very much committed to the existing economic and political systems. But he felt they needed reforms which would enable them to survive.

Keynes was not a nationalist in the narrow sense of the word. His brand of patriotism was international in outlook, and embraced monetary and economic cooperation with the other leading nations.

His great legacy was the era of international co-operation which lasted from the mid 1940s to the end of the 1960s. He negotiated this chiefly with the Americans, and especially at a great conference held at Bretton Woods in the US in 1944. The message of that

Car manufacture: the level of demand for cars affects employment not only in the industry itself, but in industries supplying the raw materials and components – the steel, tyre, and electrical industries, to list but a few. (Management Today)

conference was that if individual countries, confronted with a major problem such as unemployment, tried to act on their own, they would only make things worse for everybody else. As an example, the protection of UK industry by limiting imports might help jobs here, but would harm jobs in foreign countries. Those countries would then retaliate and protect their own industries, harming job prospects in UK export industries. Thus, in the end, we would *all* be worse off. Keynes argued, therefore, that all countries should act together and maintain employment jointly.

The importance of demand
The Keynesian diagnosis of unemployment is simple – deceptively so. A person will not be employed unless his services, the sort of things he does using his skills, are demanded. Services will be demanded if the thing or things they are used to produce are in turn demanded (or expected to be demanded in the not too distant

future). As an example, the demand for steel workers depends on the demand for steel. But it is obvious that the demand for steel does not exist for its own sake. It too will depend on there being a demand for what it is used for - things like motor cars. So the demand for motor cars influences employment not only in the motor industry, but also in the steel industry.

It requires not a lot of imagination to see that the jobs available in the economy as a whole depend in a general way on the demands for all the goods and services that can be produced. This is sometimes referred to as aggregate demand. It is a major contribution of Keynesian economics to say:
- positively: total employment depends on aggregate demand
- negatively: if employment is too low (i.e. there is unemployment) this is because aggregate demand is too low.

This is simple and straightforward, but it has one consequence which is even more remarkable. The people who are employed earn an income. Some of that income is taxed away. Most of what is left they spend - i.e. they demand goods and services. But we have already pointed out that demand for goods and services leads to jobs. Putting the two sets of ideas together, we can say that *employment* gives rise to income, which gives rise to demand for goods and services, which gives rise to *employment*. But if too few people are in jobs demand will be too low, causing the low level of *employment* to persist. Most importantly, we can break into this logical structure at another stage: higher demand for goods and services leads to more people in jobs and higher income sustaining the higher demand.

We can get higher demand by cutting taxes. That leaves people with more income after tax. They spend and create more jobs.

We can also get higher demand by raising government expenditure. That spending is itself a demand for goods and services and yet again creates more jobs.

The government often tells us that as a country we cannot spend in the long run more than we earn. A

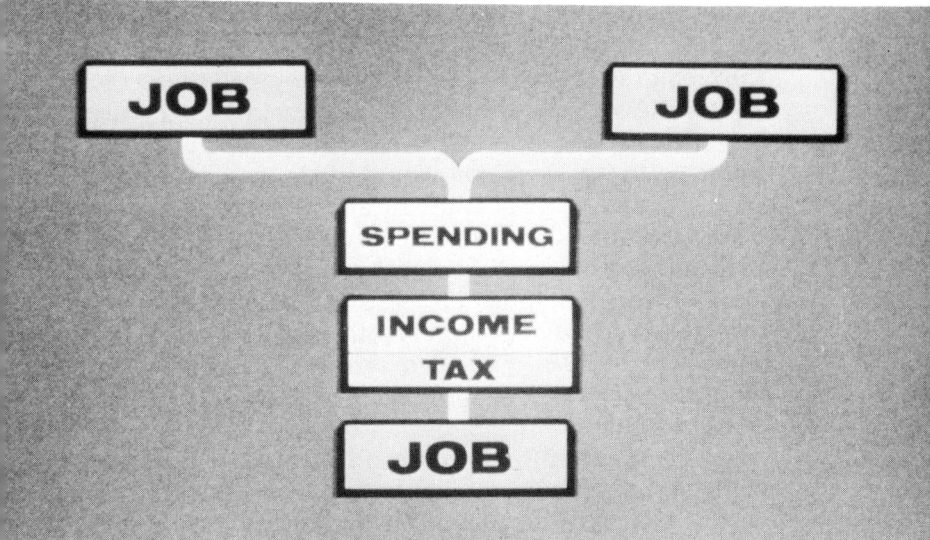

A job provides income, which is taxed. Income is spent, providing more jobs. The government can use the tax it receives to create further jobs, financed by government spending.

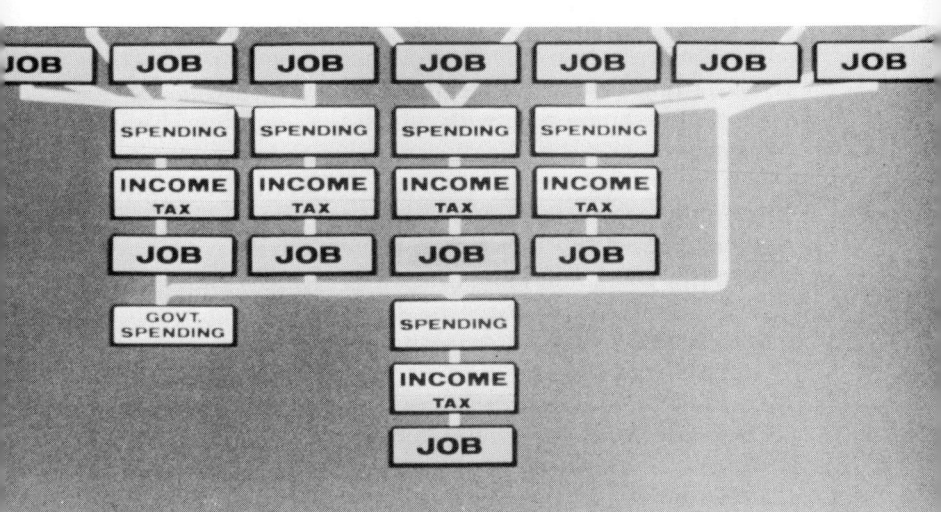

major Keynesian contribution is to turn this on its head and state that it is equally true that we cannot earn more than we spend!

This message about the effects of demand being too low is confirmed fully by various surveys of business opinion. It is well known that businessmen are currently extremely pessimistic about the future both of their own firms and the country as a whole. At the present time the key factor depressing them is lack of demand for their products. Most businessmen would sell more and produce more if only the customers were there. In addition, if the demand were higher permanently, that would restore their confidence, and they would gradually take on more workers.

The message of Keynesianism is, therefore, first and foremost one of demand, or spending. If there is too little employment, the reason is that spending is too low. If the question is asked, 'When will we return to full employment?', the answer is, 'When demand is raised sufficiently to warrant the taking on of the whole of the available labour force.' When I say 'available', I mean willing and able to work at the going rate of pay and conditions corresponding to their skill, ability, and experience.

How can demand be raised? One answer is to increase the amount of income that people have to spend. This can be done by cutting taxes, leaving wage earners with more take-home pay, with which they will buy things. Similarly, social security payments can be raised.

Another answer is based on the point that a lot of spending is financed by borrowing. This is true of home purchase, of the purchase of such durable goods as refridgerators and cars, and, above all, the machinery and equipment required by business. If you make it cheaper to borrow by lowering the rate of interest that will encourage spending.

A third answer is to note that the government can and does spend directly itself. It can take people on itself, by expanding the health service or education, for example, or it can build more roads or housing, encouraging private firms to take on more employees. Even if the government takes people on its payroll, it helps the private sector, for, as we have already seen, the people will spend their incomes creating profits and employment for others.

No Keynesian has ever argued that demand is *all* that matters or that unemployment is the *only* economic problem. But demand matters very much, and unemployment is a terrible social evil and economically extremely wasteful. Three million unemployed imply an economic loss of £20 billion to £30 billion *every year*. That is an estimate of how much extra output could be produced if the unemployed were found jobs. That output is lost forever.

Economic progress requires a trained labour force, and, more to the point, a retrained one as technology changes, but there is no sense in devoting a great effort to training if there is no demand for what the people can do when they are qualified. Clearly, some people may be unemployed because they have the wrong skills. But, in helping them to acquire new skills, it is also necessary to keep spending buoyant so that what those skills produce is wanted.

The same point applies to job search and encouraging people to be mobile. Something has to be done to increase the number of available jobs, which again takes us back to demand.

If demand is so important, why, in Britain does the present Conservative government not do something about it? The answer to this is partly because of its political views and prejudices. The present government has committed itself to something which is called monetarism. Curiously enough, one leading monetarist has denied that this government's policies are truly monetarist, but it is not for the rest of us to get involved with doctrinal nitpicking, especially those of us who believe that monetarism is absurd in the first place.

Essentially, monetarism amounts to the belief that the economy is automatically self-righting, i.e. it guarantees full employment if left to itself. This means that the government can do nothing at the macroeconomic level to bring us full employment or to keep us

'A city of skills ...' But are the skills the ones needed? Retraining may be necessary to provide a workforce with skills that are needed. 'But, in helping them to acquire new skills, it is also necessary to keep spending buoyant so that what those skills produce is wanted.' (Network; Polytechnic of Central London)

A Keynesian View

there. The government can make things worse and can cause inflation, but, if it refrains from doing that, all will be well.

Of all the many reasons why monetarism is a mistaken doctrine, the most important is that it does not fit the facts. Experience shows that, left to itself, the economy does not automatically head for or stay at full employment.

It is not even the case that the monetarists' favourite policy - controlling the money supply to remove inflation - works at all easily or lowers the rate of price increase without adding considerably to the numbers unemployed. This is shown by the British experience.

The effect of monetarist policies in the United Kingdom in the three years up to 1982 has been to add about one and a half millions to the numbers unemployed. Far from assisting growth, output at the end of 1981 was some five per cent lower than it was in 1978 and manufacturing output has gone down by more than ten per cent. Even the rate of price increases has not yet fallen much below what it was when the experiment started. Above all the effect of the policies has been to damage future prospects compared with the improvement that would have been possible.

Setting the monetarist heresy on one side, why then would the government - any government - hesitate before acting? Why not cut taxes and increase public expenditure to get us back to full employment? There are a great many reasons why the path back to full employment must be a slow and tough one.

One obvious reason is that a large part of the goods we buy in this country come from abroad, while a lot of what we produce is exported. An increase in British demand, therefore, will flow abroad to a considerable extent, and create jobs for foreigners, not ourselves. We need foreign demand for our goods to rise, but the British government cannot do a lot about that on its own. That is why Keynesian economists have argued for a policy of joint expansion of demand by all governments together.

One thing we can do is to devalue our currency, i.e. to

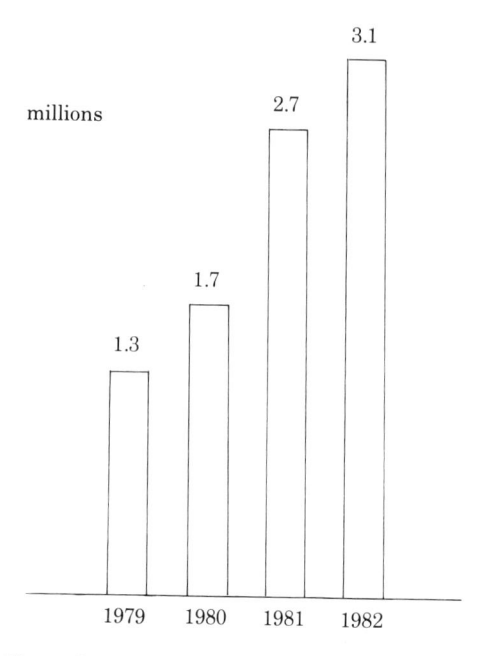

Figure 7. Unemployment in Britain (millions).

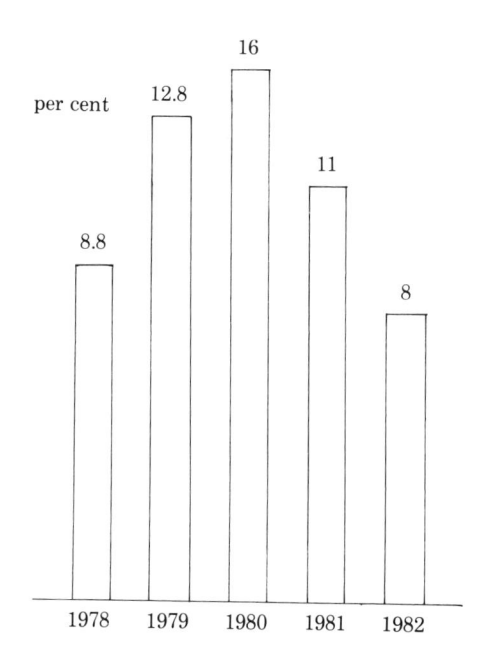

Figure 8. Inflation in Britain (Retail Price Index, year on year, percentage increase).

A Keynesian View

make pounds cheaper in terms of foreign currencies. This means that British goods will appear cheaper to foreigners and they will buy more of them. It also means that foreign goods will appear dearer to us, causing us to import less and switch more of our demand to our own sources of production.

There are many complications that arise with devaluation. One that we must emphasise immediately is that it *does* raise the price of imports, and is, therefore, inflationary.

This leads us on to the whole question of extra spending and inflation. Suppose there is unemployment, and the government acts to raise demand. Will it necessarily lead to more output and more employment?

There are two circumstances under which it will not. One is when employers, finding that they are able to sell more, choose instead to raise their prices, making more profit on a constant level of sales. A second is when employees, appreciating that their services are needed more, insist on higher money wages than would otherwise be the case. This makes it less profitable to take on more workers and again means the demand will be dissipated in higher prices. In both cases expanding demand raises prices (i.e. increases inflation) without helping employment much.

Keynesians have always acknowledged that, when demand expands, it leads to a rise in prices as well as output and employment. But they have insisted that with large scale unemployment the effect on prices and wages would be small. That was Keynes's view in the 1930s as long as unemployment was above 5 per cent. Up to 1970 it was felt by most economists that inflation did not become a serious problem until unemployment fell below 2 per cent.

Events in the 1970s indicated that they may have been over-optimistic in this. Even with three million unemployed, workers are still fighting vigorously for higher pay. It is believed by many, therefore, that expansionary policies could be defeated by more inflation.

Therefore, Keynesians nowadays typically advocate

incomes policies as part of an expansionary strategy. What this means is that money incomes must be restrained. It does not mean that real take-home pay must necessarily be cut for all workers. That depends on how much more output the additionally employed workers produce as well as on possible tax reductions. (Do not forget, in considering economic expansionary measures, what the effect of this policy will be on the government's finances. There is a great deal saved on unemployment pay and social security benefits. And, of course, the newly employed pay taxes on their incomes, and VAT on what they buy.)

Even with tax cuts, higher real government spending, and an incomes policy, progress must still be slow. It takes time for additional workers to be recruited, to be fitted into the production programme, and for some of them to acquire new skills. Because of the extent and depth of the depression, equipment has become obsolete and needs to be renewed and added to.

Above all, employers need to be persuaded that any increase in real demand will be sustained. Otherwise, it will not be worthwhile for them to take on new workers with all the costs that that involves. (They have to consider the cost of future redundancy payments if they misjudge the scale of the boom). It will also not be worthwhile for them to increase their stock of machinery. Machines last a long time, and it is only profitable to acquire them if the demand for the goods they produce also lasts a long time.

The reason why the economy did so well up to the end of the 1960s was that it was expected to do well. Employers were confident that they could sell what they produced. Any setbacks were regarded as temporary – they would be self-righting or sorted out by the government.

A policy for full employment
The tragedy of the last decade is the destruction of confidence. Employers and employees no longer believe in real expansion. And, if the economy ever got going again, they do not trust the government to keep it going.

A Keynesian View

The *expectation* now is for stagnation and inflation – that unlikely combination called stagflation.

That is the reason why a Keynesian expansion policy has to be slow but sure. It must restore confidence in a sustained and sustainable expansion of real demand, in both the public and private sectors, without adding to inflation. It is, therefore, to be built on four legs:

- tax cuts
- more public spending
- incomes policy
- devaluation.

Tax cuts may themselves be of many different kinds, and economists are not agreed on their effects. There are those who favour cuts in income taxes on the grounds that these would give an incentive to people to work harder. But some economists have pointed out that this tax cut may be a *disincentive* to effort since workers would get the same after-tax income for less work. They, therefore, favour a cut in VAT which is a tax on expenditure and would imply lower prices and an apparently lower inflation rate.

It is also worth noting that national insurance contributions are a tax. Those paid by employers are essentially a tax on taking on more workers. If the employers' national insurance contributions were reduced, there would be a direct encouragement to take on more employees.

On public spending, the range of options is even larger. Should increases be on health, or education, on roads or factories, on police or the armed services, on old age pensions or high unemployment pay? A case can be made for any or all of these, so priorities have to be established. But there is also the question of the nature of the expenditure. If education is to be helped, how should the money be divided between more teachers, more books, and more buildings? In health, is the priority to be given to more doctors and nurses, more equipment, or new hospitals? In all these cases, the fundamental point must not be missed: a decision to spend on equipment or buildings or roads still encourages employment, because people have to be taken on to make such things.

What about an incomes policy? If it is feasible at all, there is still a range of possibilities to be examined. There may simply be a norm for the public sector which may be a flat rate increase (e.g. £5 per week for everyone) or a percentage increase (e.g. 5 per cent for everyone) or a combination of the two. The norm may be extended to the private sector with penalties for firms who break it and/or subsidies to firms who stick to it. Coupled with incomes restraint, there may be price restraint, especially to hold back price rises from firms who possess strong monopoly power. An incomes policy might be agreed with the official trades union movement, although, given the recent pronouncements of their leaders, that seems rather optimistic. Alternatively, it may be imposed by the government, with or without a legal back-up. This is essentially what the Conservative government has done with respect to pay in the public sector. It has tried to impose a limit on the wages it is willing to pay its own workers. But whatever is done, action is required urgently even though it can only be modest in scale.

To succeed, the chosen policies must involve a commitment of no less than five years, and probably more like ten. They are not all that is needed. They must be supported, especially in the area of training and research and development, to raise productivity. But a sustained real expansion of demand is an essential ingredient for success.

It would be helped enormously if other countries expanded too. As long as action is not delayed, it might also be a good idea to call together a conference of the major world economies so that they can act jointly, as they agreed to do when they met at Bretton Woods nearly four decades ago. But it is vital that matters are not allowed to drift.

For the UK, my own view is that we need to:
- cut the employers' national insurance contribution
- cut income tax
- raise current expenditure on health and education

A Keynesian View

- increase the rate of road, factory and house building
- institute an incomes policy involving both a flat rate and percentage element
- control prices set by monopolies.

This is a policy package that would succeed. The result would be a gradual return to full employment with no worsening of inflation. We would all get back to work and our standard of living would start to rise again.

SAM AARONOVITCH

A Marxist View

The world is in deep recession and it is no secret that Britain's problems are worse than those of many industrial countries. Some people believe that the responsibility for this rests on a single person - Margaret Thatcher. They see her as a fanatical bigot leading Britain to disaster for the sake of an irrational dogma called monetarism. You may expect me, a Marxist, to go along with Mrs Thatcher's critics.

I do believe that Tory policy has done great damage, but as I see it, Thatcherism is not simply an irrational dogma. It is a serious attempt by powerful circles in big business and the Tory party to cope with the cumulative effects of Britain's decline over the last century.

Some people see the causes of the present crisis in the recent past. They put it down to the rise in oil prices, or to rapid technological change. But I believe we must look for the causes of this crisis a lot further back.

As we enter the 1980s we can see how the long recession of the 1930s gave way to World War II. The war gave way to a long boom, and the boom has given way to another long recession. All the industrialised countries are in crisis, and the effects of it reach across the entire world.

But Britain has done worse than other industrial countries, as all the figures show. Our unemployment is higher than in any other industrial country, our output has fallen more sharply than in other countries, and the cost of this in economic and human terms is enormous.

That is what we see on the surface, but we have to dig deeper to understand what is happening to Britain. We have to take a much more fundamental look at what makes the capitalist system tick.

A Marxist View

Capitalism and crisis

I say 'capitalist system', because I think that most people would agree that Britain, along with countries like the US, West Germany and Japan are 'capitalist societies' in the sense that things like factories as well as banks and insurance institutions are in the main privately owned and controlled. That is important, because it means that the surplus from what is produced and sold becomes the property of these private owners.

Think of capitalism as the latest and most advanced form of 'class society'. Now class societies develop when those who work are capable of producing a surplus over and above their own needs. The history of different kinds of society is also the history of the different ways in which this surplus is produced and shared out.

In *slave* society, for instance, the slaves were owned by the slave owners, so whatever the slave produced belonged to the slave owners.

In *feudalism,* the lords either owned or controlled the land, and the serfs had to hand over part of what they produced on their holdings or work directly for the lord of the manor.

In *capitalism,* the workers do not own the factories (the means of production) so they must work for those who do.

Capitalists are those who own or control the means of production and so own and control what is produced, however little they have done to produce it. In capitalism, speaking simply, the surplus product produced is roughly the same as what is generally called 'profit'. As we all know, the driving force of capitalism is just this – to produce a profit. Each group of capitalists believes its survival hangs upon its ability to make a profit, and then re-invest that profit to make more profit – in other words to carry through a process of profitable *expansion*. And the push towards profitable growth is really the driving force of capitalism. This gives capitalism a dynamism that no previous society ever had.

But what are the consequences? Every capitalist tries

to increase productivity, to bring in new machinery and to increase the intensity of labour. They try to find new markets, to stimulate demand for their products, to find new sources of raw materials, to look for ever cheaper labour, and overcome the cost of rivalry by knocking out or absorbing competitors. And this is how economic power becomes concentrated in fewer and fewer hands.

In Britain, for instance, by the mid 1970s, about eighty per cent of the assets of industrial and commercial companies were in the hands of the hundred largest companies. In manufacturing, the

'Capitalism does not only grow. It is a system of boom and slump.' (Network)

hundred largest firms account for over forty per cent of all output. Fifty per cent of Britain's exports now come from just a hundred firms.

This concentration of ownership and control happens not only in industry and commerce, but also in the financial system, both in Britain and elsewhere. Another important result of the drive for profit is that capitalists invest internationally, splitting up work between different factories in different countries,

A Marxist View

linking the world closer and closer together through the flow of trade and investment.

But capitalism does not only grow. It is a system of boom and slump. The slumps happen because, for all kinds of reasons, the conditions for profitable expansion break down. Capitalist production is aimed at making money, not at meeting human needs; so goods are produced for people who have money to buy them.

Of course, every capitalist would like those who buy their products to have plenty of money, but at the same time every capitalist would like to cut the cost of wages so that the profits are greater. But if all capitalists pay lower wages, then workers do not have enough money to buy the capitalists' products, and there is less demand for their goods.

So it is not enough for workers to make goods that *could* make a profit. Those goods have to be sold to realise that profit. And that depends on the state of the market. The problem for capitalism is that the conditions in which profits can be produced conflict with the conditions in which profits can be realised.

The Marxist calls it a crisis of over-production; suddenly there is too much 'capital'. Unemployment grows and that weakens the unions. So this crisis has a purpose, because it shakes out under-used or outdated factories, and makes it easier for capitalists to control their workers. In this way the crisis purges the system and helps to restore the right conditions for profitable expansion. For a Marxist, this explains what the present prolonged crisis in the world economy is all about.

Why is the British crisis worse?
To understand Britain's difficulties, we must go a bit further; we need to explain why Britain's problems are worse than other industrialised capitalist countries. Why have we been hit harder, fallen further behind than other countries?

When you think about it, we are not a poor country. We have energy, oil and coal. We have an efficient agriculture. We have a capable trained workforce. And

'Important sections of our industry are being knocked out before our very eyes ... '

we have a capacity for research and invention which in the past has been envied by many other countries in the world.

Yet we have low levels of investment. We have low productivity from the investment that we do carry through. Important sections of our industry are being knocked out before our very eyes.

So why? What is the reason for Britain's decline. And how did it come about?

Just over a century ago Britain was the most powerful industrial nation in the world. At that time Britain produced over forty per cent of the world output of manufactured goods entering into world trade; and accounted for thirty per cent of world trade in foodstuffs and raw materials. Britain was the greatest commercial power with a quarter of international trade passing through UK ports. But in Europe and America our rivals were fast catching up.

There were two choices for British capitalism. First, it could undertake a massive programme of modernisation to keep ahead of its rivals. Secondly, it could stake

... yet, 'just over a century ago Britain was the most powerful industrial nation in the world ... Britain was the greatest commercial power, with a quarter of international trade passing through UK ports.' (Mary Evans Picture Library)

Britain's future on maintaining a role as a world power by pursuing imperial expansion to corner markets in colonies such as India; by pushing for free trade elsewhere in the world; by acting as the world's shipper, insurer, and trader; and by developing Britain as a financial centre for the world economy, with the pound sterling as the lynch pin. It took the second option. By 1913 more capital was already being invested abroad than in the UK.

It could be argued that those who ruled Britain were prisoners of their own history. Nevertheless, time and again over the last hundred years their actions meant that Britain's national industrial base was sacrificed to what they saw as Britain's world role and world interests.

It happened in the 1880s when Britain's lead was being challenged seriously for the first time. It happened in the 1900s, when Britain stuck to free trade whilst rivals were protecting their home markets.

It happened in the 1920s when Churchill at the Treasury chose to restore the gold standard and overvalued the pound. It happened in the 1950s when Gaitskell sacrificed major export chances to double the arms programme, at the request of the United States. And it happened in the 1970s when Healey opted to defend the pound sterling by cracking down hard on the British economy.

Each time, Britain's leaders chose the defence of sterling, the defence of free trade, and the vision of Britain as a world power. The combination of these three things was a recipe for economic suicide, because the very thing that strengthened the international role of the City of London weakened Britain's national industrial development.

As our rivals grew in strength and became more active in world trade, sterling became the vital means of financing that trade, and this in turn made the City of London even more a centre of the world economy. To keep the City of London at the centre of the world economy became more crucial than building up Britain's industrial base.

Five men with a vision of Britain as a world power. Have the consequences of that vision irreparably damaged Britain's industrial base? Clockwise from top left: Gladstone (Chancellor of Exchequer 1852, Prime Minister 1868-74, 1880-86 and 1892-4); Asquith (Prime Minister 1908-16); Gaitskell (Chancellor of Exchequer 1950-51); Churchill (Chancellor of Exchequer 1924-9; Prime Minister 1940-45, 1951-5); Healey (Chancellor of Exchequer 1974-9) (All BBC Hulton Picture Library)

Munitions production. The two World Wars masked Britain's economic decline, both because its competitors were knocked back and because the needs of war stimulated production. (BBC Hulton Picture Library)

Whenever there was a threat to the value of the pound sterling, British Governments cracked down on the economy by cutting back on demand, by deflation. This discouraged productive investment at home and so further weakened the ability of the British economy to compete with other countries.

Britain's rulers opted to restore the confidence of international investors, and to prop up the value of the pound at the price of sacrificing the British economy. So the British financial system was very much directed abroad, whilst at home finance and industry were kept at arm's length. And the belief in free trade strengthened the idea that the British state should not be involved in the industrial side of the economy.

Consider how different things were in Germany and Japan. There, government and banks combined to

A Marxist View

build up a powerful and advanced industrial base, using protection when they thought it necessary.

This is a root cause of Britain's economic decline. It was masked by the effect of two world wars, in each of which Britain's rivals were knocked back. With peace, the rivalry returned and the downward spiral began again.

The consensus, Thatcher and Keynes

So far, I have been discussing Britain's *relative* decline compared to other industrial countries. The British economy has continued to grow, and in absolute terms grew faster since 1945 than at almost any other time in its history. We benefited from the world-wide expansion in trade. We had practically full employment and this leads me to a major point.

Marxists place a lot of weight on class relationships and, in particular, on the relationship between capital and labour. It is obvious that when there is full employment, the working class and the trade union movement have greater bargaining power, and they use that bargaining power to ensure that working people gain a bigger share of the wealth produced. But the labour movement in Britain has never really challenged the system as a whole. It had no serious alternative vision of what British society ought to be like, so it has basically been defensive. Fundamentally, it accepted that it would operate within the framework of the system as it was.

In its turn, the leadership of the Tory Party acknowledged the existence of this powerful labour and trade union force and adopted a policy of consensus (of 'don't rock the boat') as a way of maintaining the stability of the system.

But by the late 1970s this kind of 'working agreement' had become a liability, not only in the eyes of the left of the Labour Party but, more importantly, in the eyes of powerful groups within business and the Tory Party. They became increasingly impatient at the ability of the trade unions to get in the way of Tory government policy.

'May they ever be united.' This Victorian Trade Union banner suggests the acceptance by the labour movement of the 'working agreement' with employers. (John Gorman)

It was Margaret Thatcher who led the Tory Party towards right-wing radical policies to break up this consensus.

From a Marxist point of view, Thatcherism represents an attempt by big business and finance to restore the right conditions for profitability, to carry out a partial modernisation of Britain's economy. To carry

A Marxist View

this through means breaking the bargaining power of the trade union movement - or to put it another way, shifting the balance of power between capital and labour even further towards capital. It is no surprise, therefore, that Thatcher's policies have made the economic crisis worse. Inflation has come right down. But at what price?

In three years, the home market for manufactured goods has fallen by 16 per cent. Manufacturing investment has fallen by 30 per cent. Manufacturing output has fallen by 15 per cent, more than in the great depression of the 30s, and far more than any other industrial country. At the end of 1981, the current cost of unemployment was a staggering £15 billion a year, equal to £4,500 a year for every single employed person.

In fact, Thatcher's monetarist policies have only achieved a partial modernisation. People are being made to work harder - those who still have jobs - but the fall in investment and research means that, except in some areas, equipment and technology are not being substantially advanced.

Thatcherism has weakened the British economy and helped bring mass unemployment. And in order to deal with the social and political consequences of all this, Thatcherism, far from rolling back the power of big government, has had to strengthen the power of the state, increasing the hardware of the armed forces and the police. A weak economy needs a strong state.

It is hardly surprising that this experience of monetarism should have led a lot of people to look back again at the Keynesian economic approach, adopted by post-war government. Keynes showed that, in capitalist societies, there was no automatic mechanism to ensure that people (ordinary consumers and businessmen) had enough money to keep the workforce fully employed; businessmen will not invest if they do not think they can sell the extra output at a profit they find acceptable. But in turn, if investment declines, so do profits; and that leads to even less investment and so also more unemployment.

Keynesians say that if there is unused labour and

'A weak economy needs a strong state'. (Press Association)

unused resources, the state should spend to bring this labour and these resources into use again - in other words, reflation. And if the government reflates, then businessmen produce and invest more to meet this increased demand.

Keynesian ideas were useful to both government and business in justifying state intervention. But it also brought them problems, because, whilst a high level of demand leads to a high level of employment, it also increases the bargaining power of workers. It also increases state spending on social services, which means higher levels of taxation. More fundamentally, if the state were given more leverage in the economy, then in a country like Britain with a powerful trade union and labour movement there was always the possibility that a Labour government might use this state power to make far more radical changes.

In fact Keynesianism hardly begins either to tackle the underlying causes of Britain's relative decline or to ensure that expansion continues.

The Labour Party and the TUC have put forward an Alternative Economic Strategy. The 1981 'Peoples' March for jobs' shows their concern. (Network)

What is to be done?

We need a massive programme for expansion. We need a large-scale programme for creating new jobs and of training and education of the sort the Labour Party and the TUC have put forward. But do we want just any kind of growth? No matter what it does to the environment? Do we want just any kind of jobs, even if they are all devoted to making arms for export?

It is not just a question of 'regenerating the economy', but of what kind of regeneration, and in whose interests.

That is why I believe that the revitalising of Britain's economy, in a way that meets the needs of ordinary people, cannot be carried out by those who now own and control it. It can only be done if the British people are fully involved in the major decisions both where they work and where they live.

Changing Britain means extending democracy, and

that in its turn means challenging the existing class set-up of British society. At present, ten per cent of the population own sixty per cent of the wealth in Britain. One per cent of the adults own twenty-five per cent of personal wealth. One per cent own seventy per cent of

Total private investment abroad.

private land, and seventy-five per cent of all privately owned shares.

The attempt to preserve and extend private wealth and power has closed factories and destroyed the economic livelihoods of whole communities. For if those who own or control capital think it will be more profitable to invest elsewhere, then that is where they will invest it. In that sense, 'capital' has no country. Between 1978 and 1981 total private investment abroad nearly doubled from £34 billion to £64 billion.

If all this is to be changed, there has to be a real shift in economic power, towards working people. Let us be clear: we do not have the simple choice between total planning on the one hand and the completely free market on the other. We live in a world of giant firms which plan on a world scale, and of powerful inter-

A Marxist View

vening governments. The real issues are: What kind of planning? By whom? For whom?

Because I am a Marxist, people may think that I am about to propose a Soviet-type model. In my view, the Soviet economy is not a model of democratic control and I am not suggesting that Britain goes down that road. In any case, it is not possible, and certainly not desirable, to plan an economy in detail.

What road should we take?

It is the democratically elected bodies at national and local level, the people in their communities and enterprises, who must decide where they want the economy to go and what the priorities are. I see the central and local government, together with national assemblies, concerning themselves with a limited number of major decisions about how much of the wealth created should go to investment, personal incomes and public services. They would be concerned with key investment decisions on matters like energy and high technology, decisions which shape the economy over long periods of time.

It must be obvious that we cannot move along that road without a shift in economic power: it cannot happen if Britain remains dominated by giant privately controlled multinational firms and financial institutions backed by the full force of the state.

How is this shift in power to take place? What are the first steps we need to take? To begin with there is a powerful case for the extension of public ownership.

We need public ownership to get integrated energy and transport systems and so that the benefits of North Sea oil can come to the people.

We need it to get the necessary massive spending on high technology to put the UK economy into the top league of advanced countries. We need it in banking and insurance, to make sure that the country's savings can help modernise our economy, instead of much of it going abroad, or into property, or into other financial services.

There is something ridiculous about pension funds funnelling money overseas and weakening the British economy when, after all, a strong domestic economy is the only sound foundation for looking after those who will be the pensioners of the future.

I must make it clear: I am not arguing for more autocratically run National Coal or Rail Boards. I am arguing for enterprises where industrial democracy is real, and where the communities in which they operate play a real part in making the decisions that affect their lives. Public ownership should increase people's involvement, and give democratic institutions powerful levers for change.

But notice that I have not put forward a plan for wholesale nationalisation. Whatever may happen in the long run, the greater part of farming, distribution, trading and manufacturing, and a good part of the financial services would be in the hands of privately owned companies, co-operatives, and self-employed people.

What is called 'the market' and the 'price mechanism' would play an important part, but they would be helping society to work better and not be dominating it.

Today, the hundred largest manufacturing firms produce over forty per cent of all manufacturing output, and account for much of manufacturing employment and investment, so it is important that what they do should contribute to the industrial revitalisation of the economy.

That is why I support the proposal for Planning Agreements in which central (and local) government, would work out with management and unions what the firms will do about investment, employment, output, prices and markets.

Most of the giant firms are multinational: they can play off one country against another, but even so, these companies come in many different shapes and sizes. This is one area where a systematic effort must be made to get international agreement between governments.

In an interdependent world, how can the British people have more say about their country's place in the world economy? The changes that have to take place in what we produce, export and import, must be nego-

A Marxist View

tiated, and not forced on us by decisions taken by giant firms and by other governments.

Britain needs foreign trade, to finance a growing economy and to help provide jobs. And we want to help develop countries which are now poor but could become excellent markets if they break out of their poverty traps.

Marxists completely agree that if we want such trade we must be efficient and competitive. But that means we must give our industries a chance to grow and not let them be knocked out by uncontrolled imports. It is not sensible to let capital flow freely in and out. That is why we propose the planned growth of trade and the control of capital flows. We advocate long term and mutually beneficial agreements with other countries. This would not be a 'beggar my neighbour' policy, because a growing economy would be a better market for our neighbours than a stagnant or declining one.

Of course, this programme would be easier to carry through if world trade was expanding. It is hard, as the Mitterand government in France has discovered, when your trading partners are following restrictive and deflationary policies. This means that any government trying to follow such a strategy must do everything possible to get the co-operation of other governments.

All these changes involve and depend on changes in the outlook and philosophy of the labour movement itself, and especially the trade unions.

If we increase output and productivity, if we improve living standards without increasing inflation, and if we involve people in national economic decisions, we will get sensible collective bargaining.

The proposals that I have made so far are meant to help us work towards a different kind of society where the principle that guides us in how we want to live is social benefit and not private profit. It is this principle of social benefit which should help us tackle the basic issues of how we bring up our children and how men and women can co-operate fully and on equal terms. A different view of work, a completely new approach to the way work is distributed, must be part of major changes in our society.

In our modern societies, production is more and more social; in the long run, its ownership and control must also be social and cooperative. My vision of life is completely opposed to the view that money should decide everything. And I draw that vision from roots which are deep in British history. William Morris, writer, artist, craftsman, socialist and, may I say, Marxist, almost one hundred years ago, set out what is needed to transform our society. We need, he said, 'Intelligence enough to conceive, courage enough to will, power enough to compel. If our ideas of a new Society are anything more than a dream, these three qualities must animate the majority of our working people and then, I say, the thing will be done.'

William Morris (1834-96) – 'writer, artist, craftsman, socialist and ... Marxist ... .' (BBC Hulton Picture Library)

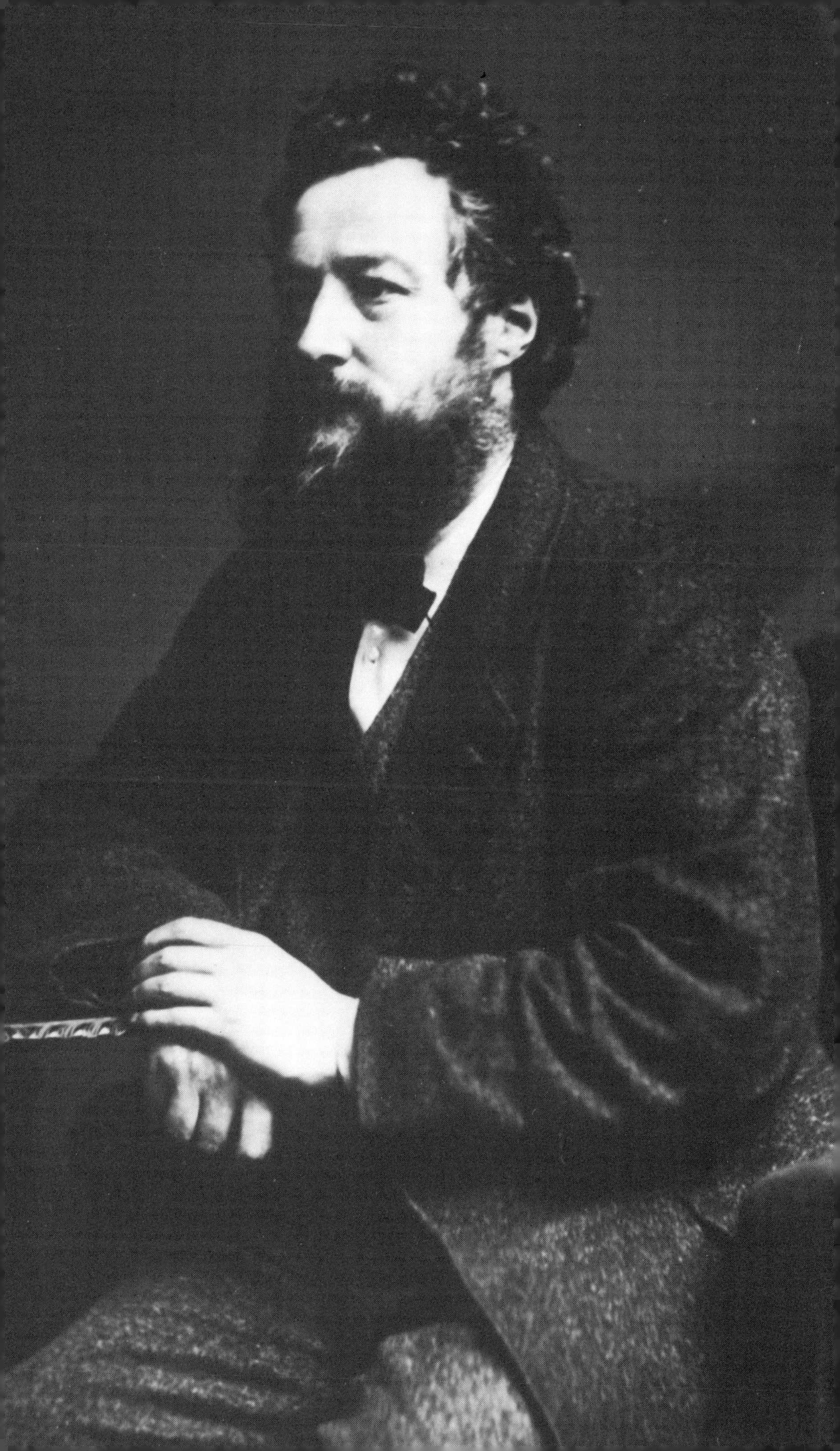

AJIT SINGH

A Third World View

If we look at the world economy today, there are two long-term developments which are of major importance. They are industrialisation in the countries of the third world, and de-industrialisation in advanced economies. I want to explore the relationship between these two: the growth of industry in the 'South' and its relative decline in the 'North'. I want to ask the question: how much of the industrial decline in rich countries like Britain is being caused by imports of cheap labour products from the Third World? And more generally, will further industrialisation of the South in the future inevitably destroy the industries of the North?

In the advanced countries, there is great concern about the problem of 'de-industrialisation'. For most people, de-industrialisation means factory closures and fewer jobs in industry and in the whole economy. In this sense, not only Britain, but most other advanced countries, have suffered from de-industrialisation over the last decade or so. Britain was among the first victims of de-industrialisation; and it is one of the most serious cases. But there have also been increasing unemployment and significantly fewer people employed in manufacturing production in almost every industrial country: in the US, Italy, France, West Germany. In the ten years between 1968 and 1978, the number of people employed in manufacturing in Britain fell by more than a million. This meant that the proportion of the labour force employed in British manufacturing dropped from 35 per cent to 30 per cent. And the same kind of decline in industrial employment was taking place in other advanced countries.

By itself, the loss of jobs in manufacturing need not be

Does industrialisation in the South cause de-industrialisation in the North? (Carlos Frier/ Alan Hutchinson; Network)

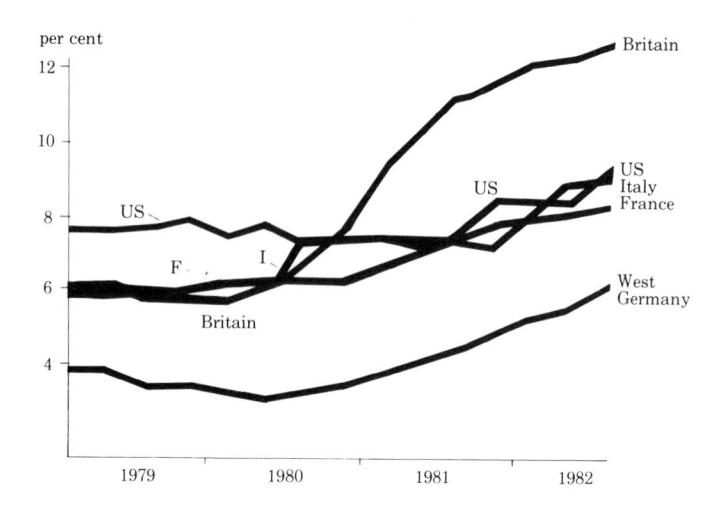

Figure 9. Unemployment: percentage of labour force, seasonally adjusted, 1979-82.

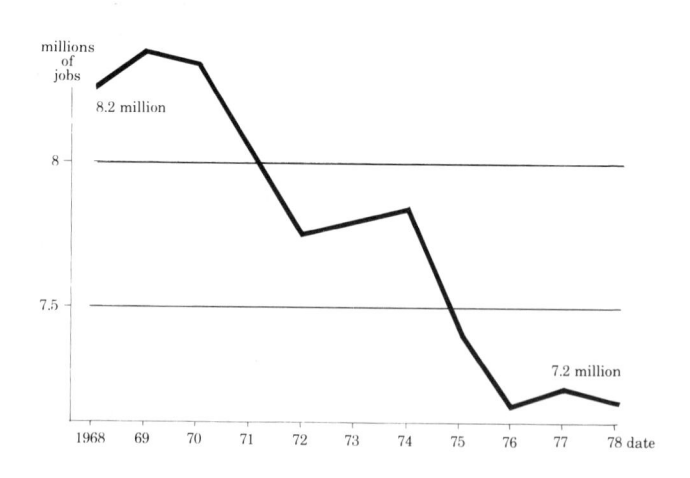

Figure 10. Manufacturing jobs in Britain.

A Third World View

a bad thing, provided that – and this is crucial – a similar number of equally, or better still, more productive jobs are being created elsewhere in the economy. If that were so, then de-industrialisation would simply reflect the normal adjustment of a modern economy to changing national and world market conditions. But de-industrialisation does become very worrying when it is not accompanied by more jobs elsewhere, but instead goes with a massive increase in unemployment. The numbers unemployed in Britain have increased from 0.5 million in 1968 to 1.4 million 10 years later in 1978, and to the present disgraceful figure of 3.3 million just 4 years on. Although unemployment has increased in other advanced countries as well, the situation in Britain is a great deal worse than elsewhere.

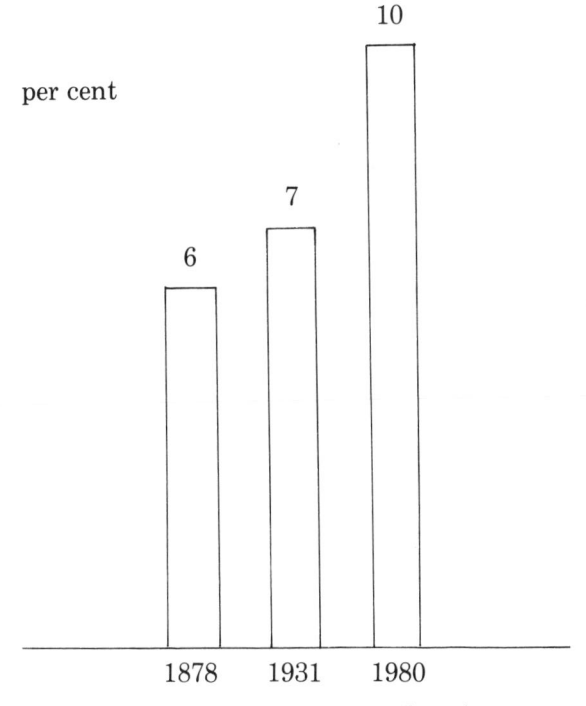

Figure 11. Decline in manufacturing output (by value, year on year) for the worst year of three recessions. The 1980s' recession is more severe than that of the 1870s or even 1930s.

The condition of British manufacturing industry has deteriorated sharply under the new so-called 'monetarist' economic policies of the Conservative government which came to power in spring 1979. The year that followed was a particular disastrous one for British industry. Historically, the fall in production during 1980 was greater than *ever* before recorded in a twelve-month period. In the Great Depression of the 1870s, the biggest annual fall was about 6 per cent in 1878. In the next Great Depression, in the 1930s, the worst year for manufacturing was 1931, when production fell by about 7 per cent. Yet in 1980, manufacturing production fell by a massive 10 per cent.

Although the industrial decline of the British economy has accelerated under Mrs Thatcher's government, the Conservatives did not create the problem. It already existed as a long-term tendency in Britain, as it did in other advanced countries. But instead of halting or reversing the process, the economic policies of the Conservative government have made the situation a great deal worse.

Now that we have well over three million unemployed – one in eight of the workforce – the economic position under the previous Labour government may seem enviable. In a way it certainly was, but we must remember that the Labour government was also unable to halt de-industrialisation, and the number unemployed, even then, was well over a million.

Industrialisation of the South
If we turn to the Third World nations of Asia, Africa and Latin America, we find most countries are experiencing acute economic difficulties at the moment, with low or declining economic and industrial growth. A very large number of them are heavily in debt, and in the present situation of world slump, they are finding it extremely difficult to meet even the interest payments on their loans. But nevertheless the *long term* record of Third World industrialisation is far from gloomy.

During the 1960s and 1970s the Third World made rapid industrial progress. Its share of world manu-

A Third World View

facturing production, though still small, rose significantly, from less than 7 per cent to over 10 per cent and it is striving to double this share, to 20 per cent by the year 2000. Some Third World countries, for example, Brazil, Mexico, India, Taiwan, Singapore, South Korea, Hong Kong – the so-called newly industrialising countries (NICs) – have been particularly successful in

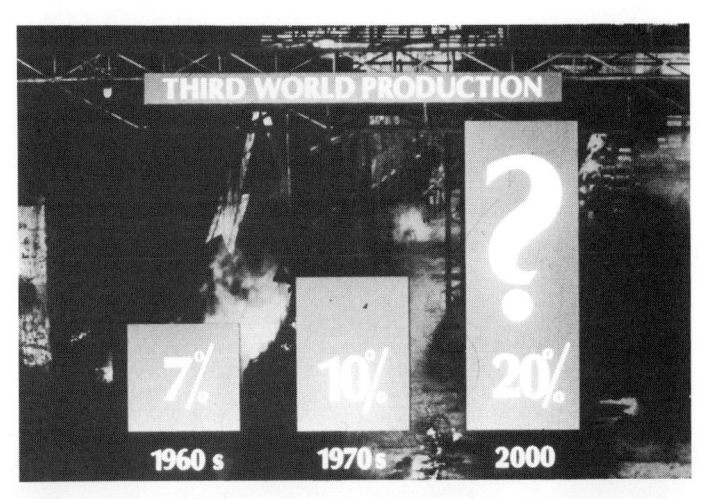

The Third World's growing share of world manufacturing production.

their industrial development. These countries are now competing with the older industrial nations, not just in labour-intensive products like textiles and footwear, but also in capital-intensive industries like steel and shipbuilding. Brazil, for example, is exporting to Europe cars, which for decades have been considered the symbol of European production. More impressively, during the past two years, Brazil has also captured a large share of the US commuter aircraft market with its small plane, the Bandit.

South Korea is now an international leader in the building of supertankers and bulk carriers, Malaysia is joining the boom in micro-electronics and computer production, and countries like India are exporting military equipment and arms, which were until recently produced by only a few advanced countries.

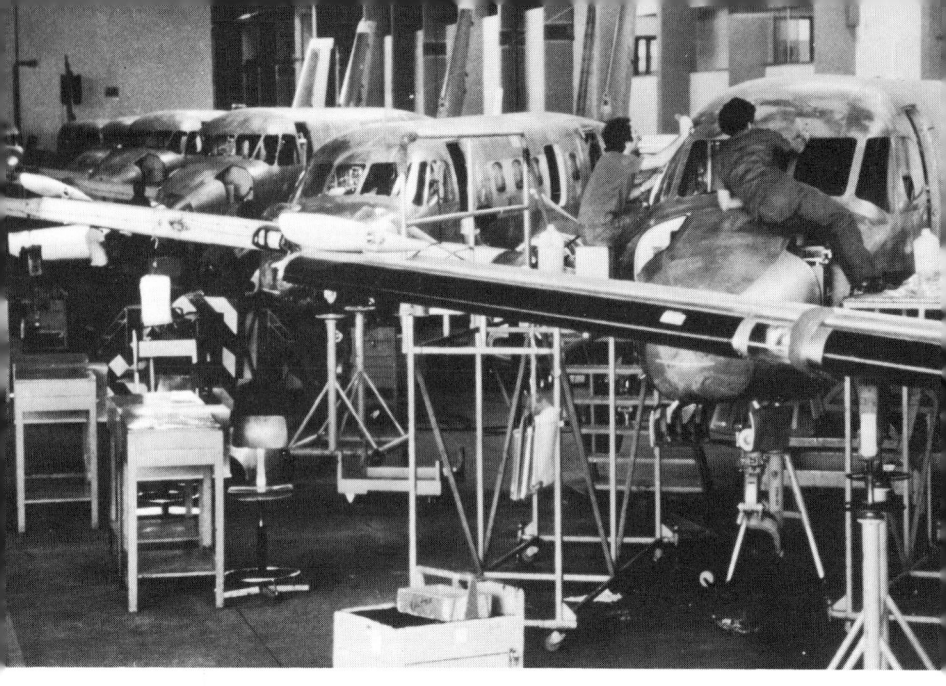

The NICs (Newly Industrialising Countries) are competing not only in low technology and labour-intensive industry, but in aircraft (Brazil) and electronics (Malaysia). (Alan Hutchinson; Malaysian High Commission)

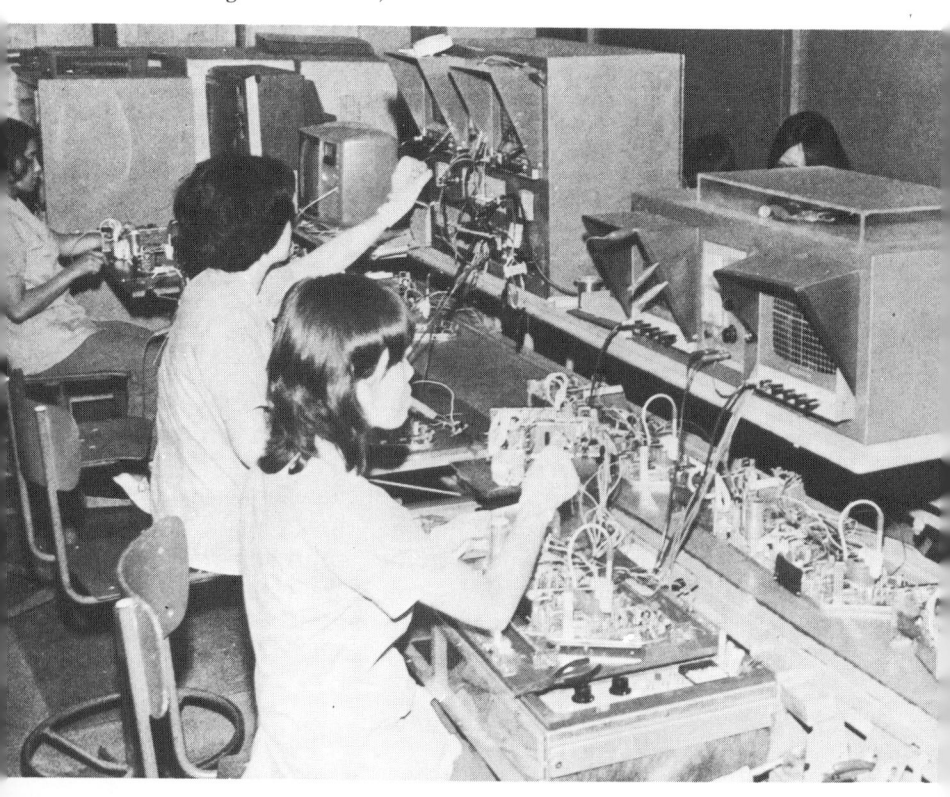

A Third World View

In 1950, only about two per cent of the world's steel was produced in Third World countries; by 1975 this had increased to over ten per cent. The Third World countries are planning to triple their steel capacity, from this level, by 1985. Meanwhile, the steel industry in the advanced countries has been facing severe difficulties; it is plagued by huge excess capacity, overproduction and declining profitability. In Britain since 1978, production has fallen by a third, and more than half the jobs in steel have disappeared. In the EEC as a whole, over the same period, nearly a quarter of the steel jobs have been lost. And in both Europe and Britain, the prospects are of further job losses and still further cuts in steel capacity. It is not surprising that the embattled EEC Commissioner of Industries has warned the developing countries bluntly 'to stop getting into manufacturing facilities, primarily steel, that provide competition for the rich world.'

The share of national output produced by a country's industrial sector is normally considered to be a very important indicator of its degree of industrialisation. One consequence of this rapid industrial development in the Third World and the de-industrialisation in countries such as Britain is that by 1981, the share of manufacturing in total output was the same in Britain as in Mexico – about 25 per cent.

In rich countries, both employers and trade unions have responded to competition from Third World countries by demanding protection for the affected industries. In one form or another – as tariffs, quotas, or the so-called 'voluntary restraints' – protective measures are being increasingly imposed on Third World manufactured exports: on steel, on textiles and on a host of other industries. Third World countries naturally object to these measures, because they reduce their rate of economic growth and also their ability to help the desperate poverty of their peoples.

The South also argues that protection against Third World manufactures not only harms the Third World, but also harms the North. For example, when the US imposes restrictions on imports of Brazilian steel, apart from anything else, it simply means that Brazil will have less foreign exchange earnings to pay interest on the debt Brazil owes to US banks. That, in the present circumstances, increases the danger of Brazil's being

Third World industrial development – today. The manufactured output is the same percentage of total output in both Britain and Mexico.

unable to repay its debt, and so threatens the stability of the world banking system.

Who is right? Is it the Northern employers and trade unionists, who every day see their factories being shut down and jobs lost to Third World imports, and therefore call for protection? Or is it the Third World countries and their supporters in the North, which today ironically include the big banks?

Why industrialise – the case of Japan
Before we tackle this question, we need to ask why the Third World countries should be so keen on industrialisation. To some people the answer will be obvious: a high material standard of living, along with a rich cultural and social life, can be produced only by a modern industrial economy. Others, however, would

A Third World View

say that it is only common sense that the South, with its large 'surplus' population, should concentrate on agriculture to feed the people, and on small scale industries to provide employment for large numbers.

Now if we look at this issue historically we find that the world has been divided broadly into two groups of countries – those which largely produce (and export) agricultural commodities, that is, the poor countries of the South, and those which largely produce manufactures, that is, the rich countries of the North.

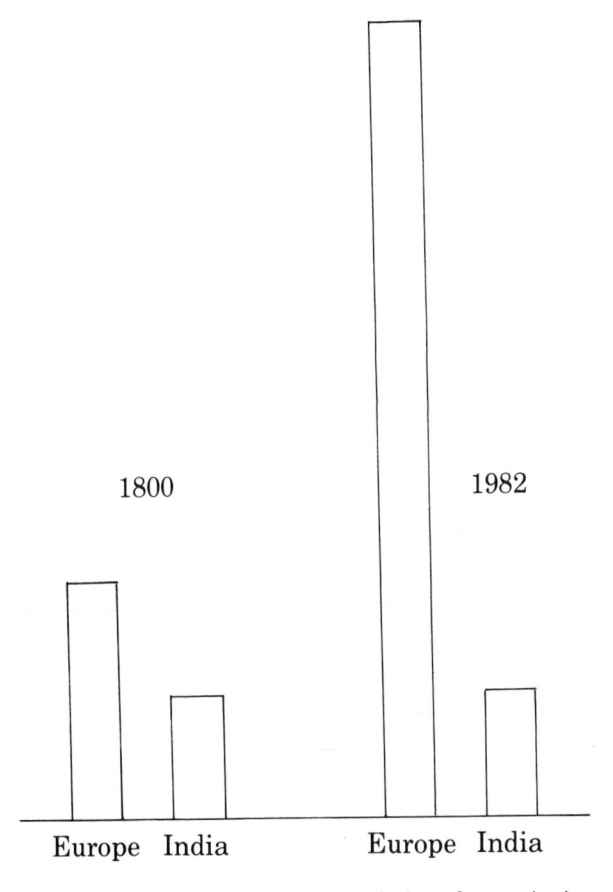

Figure 12. Diagram illustrating the relative change in incomes between North and South between 1800 and 1982. Income per head in Great Britain was twice that of India in 1800; it is now ten times.

But it is important to realise that this division of the world is a comparatively recent development, dating only from the last century or so.

Two hundred years ago, India was as important a producer and exporter of manufactured goods as Germany. In 1800, the difference between the income per head in India or China on the one hand, and Germany, France or Britain on the other, was relatively small. The average European was barely twice as rich as the average Indian. But today, the average European is *at least ten times* as rich as the average Indian.

The main reason for this change was of course the Industrial Revolution which started in Britain. After 1850, the Industrial Revolution spread from Britain to other parts of Europe, and to North America, Japan and Australia. It by-passed Third World countries like India, where, many would argue, Colonial rule slowed down or stopped industrial development in order to keep the colonies captive markets for the products of Europe.

But, today the Third World countries know that the unequal structure of the world economy can be fundamentally changed only by an industrial revolution in their own economies, even if it is rather late in the day.

Only industrialisation brings fast economic growth and reduces the technological dependence of the Third World on the advanced countries. And, in many developing countries, the key to raising productivity in agriculture *also* lies in industrialisation. It lies in the mechanisation of agriculture, and in channelling the mass of under-employed farm workers into the more productive industrial sector.

Orthodox western economists tell Third World countries that because of their advantage in cheap labour, they should specialise in labour-intensive, small-scale manufactures rather than in capital-intensive modern industry. But the Third World has before it the brilliant example of Japan. In the early 1950s, Japan, with a large population, and a high rate of unemployment, was offered a similar solution. The Japanese were told to specialise in textiles, in toys and

Industrial muscle? Japan chose high-investment industry as a long-term development plan. Osaka factory, Matsushita. (Alan Hutchinson)

their other traditional labour-intensive exports. But, the Japanese had other ideas; they deliberately and self-consciously rejected this advice. They decided to establish industries which required a great deal of capital and technology, such as steel, oil-refining, petrochemicals, automobiles, aircraft, industrial machinery of all sorts, and electronics, including computers. As a former Japanese minister has pointed out: 'In the short term, these industries would seem to make economic nonsense, but in the long term these are precisely the industries where technological progress is rapid and productivity rises fast. Without these industries it would be difficult to employ a population of a hundred million, and raise their standard of living to that of Europe.'

The important point to bear in mind here is that in the early 1950s, when Japan started on its ambitious industrial strategy, it produced only about five million tons of steel, and its level of industrialisation was lower than it is today in countries like Brazil, Mexico or even India. Each of these three countries, in 1980, produced

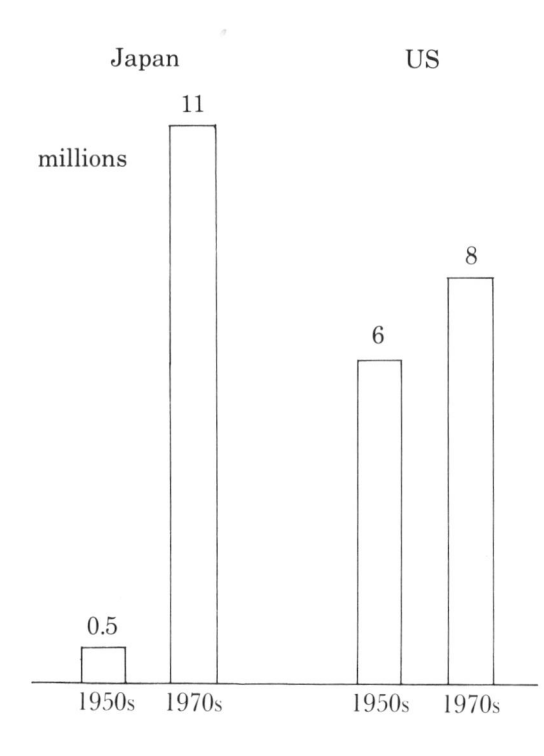

Figure 13. Car production, Japan and United States, in millions, 1950s and 1970s.

Below: The rapid growth of high-technology industry such as steel.

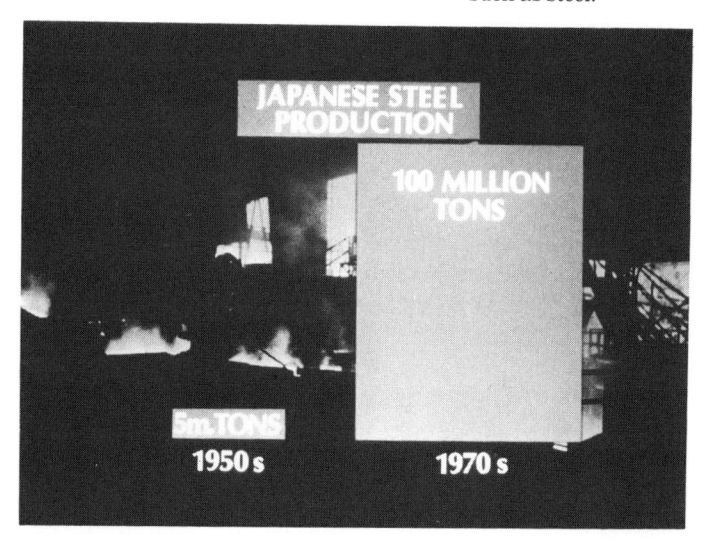

about twice the amount of steel which Japan did in the early 1950s. It is also notable that at that time, the Japanese costs of producing steel were twice the world price. Yet in the space of only twenty years, steel production in Japan had risen from five million tons to over one hundred million tons; a country which has to import all the raw materials needed for making steel has become the world's most efficient producer.

The car industry tells a similar story. On the face of it, the orthodox economic advice to the Japanese, in the 1950s, that they should produce toys or textiles rather than cars looks very sensible. How could they possibly hope to compete with the US in cars? In the mid '50s Japan produced 50,000 passenger cars a year, and the US about 6 million. Yet it took Japan less than twenty-five years to demonstrate how utterly wrong that advice was. By 1981 Japan produced 11 million cars, 3 million more than the mighty USA.

The question that the newly-industrialising countries are asking is this: Why should they not repeat Japanese economic history over the next twenty-five years? They are starting from at least as good an industrial base as Japan did when it began its spectacular post-war industrialisation drive. Some of them, like Mexico, even have oil, which Japan did not.

A threat to the North?

Now, if we shift our focus and look at this whole question from the point of view of the nations of the North, the prospect for the future is clearly one of increased competition from the countries of the South, as the South continues its intensive industrial development. Will this ever-increasing industrialisation of the South inevitably damage or destroy industry in the North? Let us first look at Britain.

The main long-term problem of the British economy is that its industry has been increasingly losing markets. Between 1960 and 1976, Britain's share in world exports of manufactured products nearly *halved,* whilst those of her competitors (except the US) either remained the same or *increased.*

At the same time, there was also a big increase in imports into Britain. These unfavourable trends in imports and exports cannot be blamed on wages or labour costs rising faster here than in other countries. Between the mid '60s and mid '70s, because of the fall in the value of the pound, British costs and prices fell relative to those in competitor countries.

Because of the growing failure of British industry in world markets, the economy has been unable to work at its full potential. Since the late '60s, Britain's balance of payments has increasingly been going into deficit, well before full employment is reached, so that full employment becomes impossible.

Let me explain in a bit more detail what I mean by this. In the mid '60s the British economy was operating at more or less full employment – the rate of unemployment was less than 1.5 per cent. At the same time, the country's foreign payments – that's roughly the difference between total exports and imports – were just about in balance. Ten years later, in the mid '70s, we find that Britain had a sizeable deficit on its foreign payments, even though unemployment had climbed to 4 per cent of the labour force.

Normally we expect that the more unemployment there is, the lower will be the level of production and people's incomes. These two factors will reduce the country's appetite for imports, and so the balance of payments should improve as unemployment increases. But what has happened instead is that, over time, despite growing unemployment, and even despite the enormous help which Britain's trade receives from its North Sea oil, the balance of payments has been going increasingly into deficit.

Today, if the country did not have 13 per cent unemployment, but full employment, the deficit would be astronomical. Since foreigners are unwilling to give Britain an endless and ever-larger overdraft to finance this huge deficit, high levels of employment are impossible.

Now, the main reason why Britain's deficit keeps growing is that industry is fast losing its own home

A Third World View

markets as well as those abroad. During the twelve months up to June 1982, manufacturing production was barely rising at all, but imports were growing at an ever increasing rate, three or four times as fast as exports.

If the poor performance of British manufacturing industry both at home and abroad is the main cause of Britain's economic failure, to what extent is it caused by trade with the Third World? During the 1960s and 1970s, there was an enormous increase in imports of Third World manufactures into this country. But the crucial point to note is that the Third World has a healthy demand for industrial plant and equipment (precisely because of its industrialisation drive). So British industrial and military exports to the Third World have also registered a huge increase.

Look at the changes in Britain's trade balance in finished manufactures with the newly industrialising countries, and also with the advanced countries such as the original six countries of the EEC, the US, and Japan. You can see that there was a massive deterioration in Britain's manufacturing trade balance with Japan and with other advanced countries, but that over time there was a very large improvement in the balance with the NICs. (Figure 14.)

In the case of Japan, the trade balance moved from a small credit of £2.7 million in the mid '60s, to an enormous deficit of over £600 million in the late '70s. Over the same period, the balance with the newly industrialised countries improved from a little over £300 million to well over £1,000 million.

So, despite the fast pace of industrialisation in the Third World, and a large increase in their manufactured exports to Britain, Britain's trade with the NICs was leading *overall* to an *increase* in Britain's domestic output and employment, rather than to a reduction. To put it bluntly, it helped, rather than hindered. In contrast, the fall in Britain's exports to other advanced countries, and the rise in imports from them, is causing *losses* in jobs and production in Britain.

But you may be wondering why, if it is trade with the advanced countries which is responsible for Britain's

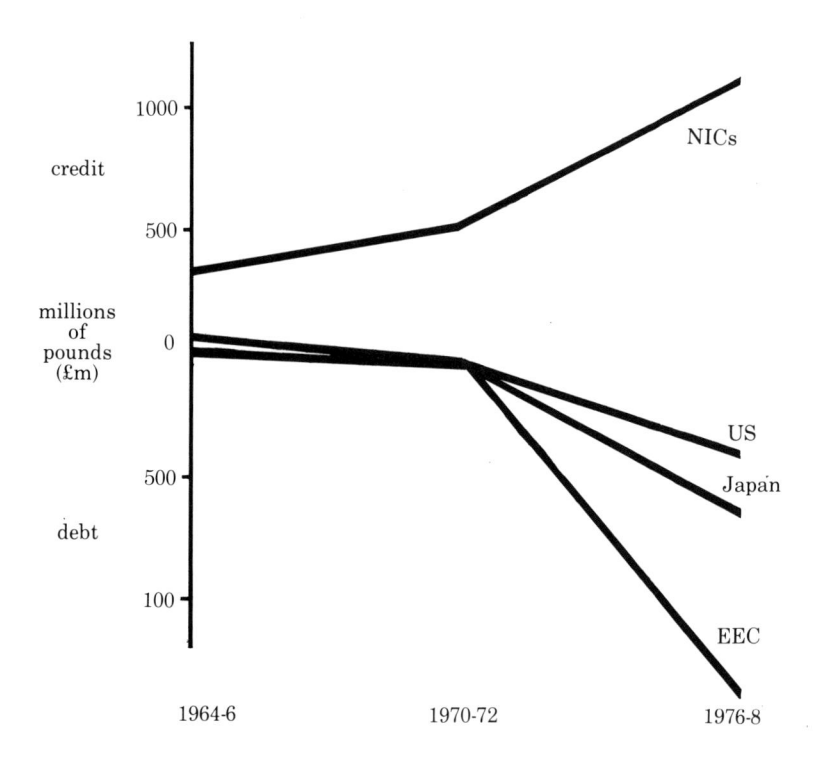

Figure 14. Diagram of British trade balance with Newly industrialising Countries and three older industrialised trading partners: the United States, Japan, and the original six members of the European Economic Community.

de-industrialisation, British industry has not been able to hold its own in the world economy? Why has British industry lost out in competition with Japan and with other advanced countries?

The British disease: unhealthy competition
People disagree about the 'original' cause of the so-called 'British disease'. Some put it down to what they call the 'laziness' of British workers, others to shortcomings of management, others to weaknesses of the education system. However, the fundamental point is

A Third World View

that, whatever the cause, once a competitive economy becomes unbalanced, this lack of balance is likely to become worse if the country continues to take part in the world economy on the same terms as before, or if it does not make the necessary changes in its production system. In a free trading system, the strong become stronger and the weak weaker; for many reasons, there may be no automatic forces to bring the economy back into 'balance', as orthodox economists often suppose.

So, if a country begins to lose its share of the world market, its firms will make smaller profits than before, leading to lower investment, less technical progress, less growth, and less ability to compete in the future. The country's products will become outdated and less and less attractive. In contrast, economies which grow quickly can achieve faster technical progress, more product innovation, and other kinds of competitive improvements.

In addition, the take-home pay of workers in a faster-growing economy will generally also be growing more quickly. This is likely to lead to better relations between workers and managers, and to benefit both productivity and performance. Because of its slow growth, British industry has suffered from both lack of technical innovation and bad labour relations. The result has been that industry is trapped in a vicious circle of decline.

So in a way, the real question is not why Britain is losing out in world markets, but rather why, despite this, Britain continues to participate in the free trading system. As an Indian economist, my original motivation for research on the problems of British de-industrialisation came from the fact that India suffered de-industrialisation in the nineteenth century. Its manufacturing industries were destroyed by competition from machine-made goods from Europe. But India was a colony at the time, and did not control its own destiny.

Why does Britain, as an independent nation, permit its industry to be destroyed by continuing to take part in a fiercely competitive free trade system?

President of France, Francois Mitterand. 'As the French expand their economy ... they immediately suck in imports.' (Frank Spooner)

De-industrialisation of the North

Finally, what about the general question of the relationship between Third World industrialisation and de-industrialisation in advanced countries? If Britain's industrial decline and rising unemployment are not due to trade with the Third World, is this also true for other advanced countries?

The answer is Yes – on the whole. Many other advanced countries have suffered from slow growth because of problems with their balance of trade in manufactured products. But these imbalances, at least up to now, have basically been due to trade amongst the industrial countries themselves, rather than to their trade with the Third World.

Take the case of France. Here we have a socialist

government, under President Mitterand, committed to full employment. The whole political programme of the French Socialist Party depends on cutting down unemployment as quickly as possible. Unlike Britain, France today has basically one of the strongest industrial economies in Europe. In addition, it has huge gold reserves. Yet the French government is finding it extremely difficult to expand the economy and to increase employment.

The reason is that since the US and other advanced economies are not growing, then as soon as the French expand their economy, in a free-trading and -financial system, they immediately suck in imports. This leads to an imbalance on foreign payments, which in turn increases pressure on the French franc to devalue, which makes inflation worse. The French trading and payments problems are clearly not being caused by South Korea or Taiwan or other Third World economies; their primary cause is France's economic relations with Germany, the US, Japan and other advanced countries.

It is of course possible that further industrialisation in Third World countries may in the future affect the balance of payments of advanced countries in the same way that today Japanese manufactures are affecting Britain and the US. But that is certainly not the situation today.

It also need not inevitably be so in the future, if different trading and financial arrangements are adopted between countries. It is worth reflecting that, during the last twenty to thirty years, there has been intensive industrialisation in one region of the world which has not harmed industrial development in the old industrial countries. Between 1960 and 1980, the centrally planned economies of Eastern Europe and the Soviet Union increased their share of world manufacturing production from 17 to 27 per cent. There is no evidence that this was at the expense of Western industrial economies. But these countries are all planned economies, and although they trade with the West, they are not an integral part of the Western free-trading system.

Summary

To sum it all up, the main question facing the newly industrialising countries of the South is how to repeat, over the next twenty-five years, the Japanese success of the last twenty-five years. The issue facing the old industrial countries of the North is how to cope, not just with one Japan, but several prospective Japans.

Given the current world slump and growing unemployment in the industrial countries it looks as if the North's system of free trade and free finance may not survive even one Japan, let alone several. But the present difficulties of the advanced countries are not due to too much trade with the future Japans but to too much unplanned trade with each other. And Britain in particular cannot hope to escape from the vicious circle by competing against the strong, while 'protecting' itself against the weak. For it is not the 'weak' countries which are harming Britain.

IRENE BRUEGEL

A Feminist View

I am going to discuss women and economics. You might well find that combination a bit strange. What I want to suggest is that much of the relationship between men and women should be seen as an *economic relationship*.

Now just suppose for a minute that Britain produced two-thirds of all the goods and services in the Common Market. And just suppose our Common Market neighbours received 90 per cent of the income and Britain got only 10 per cent. Everyone would recognise right away that that was an important economic issue. The economists and the politicians would soon be buzzing around the television studios arguing about that vast gulf between effort and reward.

But the position of men and women in the economy is similar. According to the United Nations, women in the world as a whole do two-thirds of the work and earn just 10 per cent of the income. Yet few people would recognise that as an economic issue.

Economists are in the business of comparing the economic welfare of one group against another, one country against another, and one social class against another. But they never mention that the economic welfare of one sex is greater than that of the other.

How has this situation come about? Partly because men control the economy and its image in public life. Only three of the hundred and fifty professors of economics in Britain are women. There has never been a women Chancellor of the Exchequer, and there are no women in the higher echelons of the Treasury. There are no women amongst the two hundred and fourteen directors of the twenty top companies in Britain.

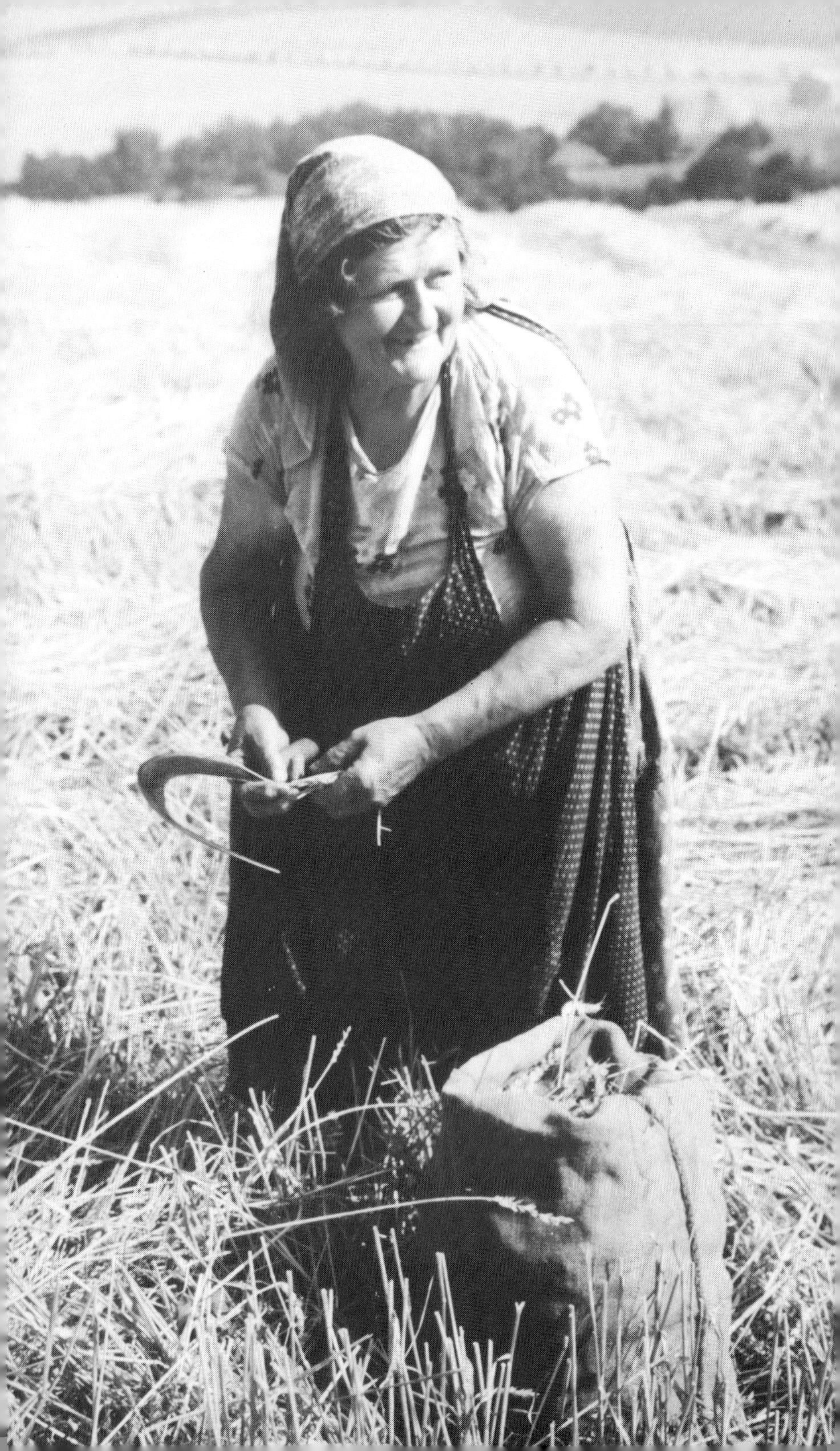

A Feminist View

Economics gives us a picture of the world as one dominated by impersonal economic forces. It is a world of competition, where the fittest survive, and where for the benefit of the majority, the weakest go to the wall. But economists coyly stop their analysis at the door of the household. Inside the home, inside the family, they paint a different picture: one where there are fair shares between people, where there is cooperation and love.

Now it would be really nice if this were the case. But when does anybody ask who in the family has the car? Who holds the cheque book? Who owns the house or holds the tenancy? If economists were prepared to ask these questions, the cosy assumption of equal sharing, of a balance between reward and effort, might well be shattered.

In fact, men get three-quarters of all the income earned in Britain and earn half as much again as women for every hour of paid work. And the tax system ensures that every married man gets a bonus – worth £575 a year in 1982 – just for being married and a man. Women, on the other hand, get left with the lion's share of the *unpaid* work.

The BBC's research on the way people spend their time shows that 162 million hours are put in to childcare, routine housework and shopping each day in Britain. Almost four-fifths of these hours are done by women.

The result is that women have much less money than men to call their own. Those who go out to work are paid less; those who work at home are paid nothing.

This is really very strange. We are told time and time again that people do not work unless they are paid, that society needs wage incentives, and that differences in pay between people are a reward for the training they have had or the extra hours they have put in. But there is a major problem with this way of thinking. Millions of housewives work hard each day and get not a penny for it. It looks as though there is one law for men and another for women.

Opposite: Two-thirds of the work ... one tenth of the income. (Network)

'In Third World countries there is no rigid dividing line between the work of growing food, selling it, and preparing it.' (J. Allen Cash Ltd)

The male bias of economics

I am not suggesting that women should be paid for housework. What I am suggesting is that this sexual division of labour is the basis for much of the sexual inequality in our society, and it should not be taken for granted.

There is a real division between work in the outside economy and work in the home. It is paid for in the one, but not in the other. But there is nothing natural or necessary in men being the breadwinners and women doing the unpaid work.

The fact that women bear children is no reason why

A Feminist View

75 per cent of obstetricians are men, or 82 per cent of secondary school heads are men. Of course many women do say that they want to stay at home to look after their children, but given the lack of alternatives in our society, they have very little real choice. Psychiatrists have found that women are far more likely to be depressed at home than they are going out to work, even though the paid work women do is often boring and soul destroying. So we cannot just accept that 'a woman's place is in the home'. In fact, this division between work in the home and work in the outside economy is a division which only really developed with the growth of industrial capitalism. Even today, in the so-called backward sectors of many Third World countries, there is no rigid dividing line between the work of growing food, for example, and preparing it; between the work of caring for children and making things for people's use.

Economists take for granted the division between the household and the outside economy. And this in turn makes the division look natural and necessary, and helps prop up the system of male advantages. In this sense, the economics we are presented with is a *male* economics.

This male bias of economics shows up in the way the health or strength of the economy is measured. It is measured by Gross National Product – GNP. But GNP does not take account of work done in the household, and, by a conservative estimate, housework is worth at least £7,000 each year per household. Measuring our economy by GNP means that only market production counts. So, when men bake bread in a bakery, that counts in GNP. But when women bake it at home – even though the bread may be a lot tastier – it does not figure officially in economic welfare.

When you buy meat, that is in the economy. When you bring it home and cook it, it is outside. When you buy a vacuum cleaner in a shop, that is an economic activity. When you use it, it is no part of the economy. Economists stop their analysis at the door of the household, and what goes on behind that closed door is another world.

This split produces a very distorted account of economic processes, for work that takes place outside the household is considered to be production, whereas the same work done inside the home comes under the general heading 'consumption'. And 'consumption' is seen as a drain on productive activity.

Now, dividing production from consumption at the door of the household may make very good sense of

Is bread making part of the GNP or not?

men's lives. They work when they are outside the home. Inside the home they *are* generally consuming. But it makes no sense of women's lives. Their activity in the home is not just consumption. They do not do the housework for fun. It is an activity necessary for the rest of the system to work. No one values a vacuum cleaner as an object in itself. Its value is in the use that housewives make of it – cleaning the house.

If production is to take place in the outside economy, there need to be workers ready and able to work. But workers do not just arise out of the blue. They are born and brought up, and educated and cared for, and fed and cleaned for by women in the home. Without this work, there would not be an economy at all. So the rigid dividing line which is drawn at the household door,

A Feminist View

between production and consumption, is misleading.

In fact, the two activities, production and consumption, are not all that it takes to make an economy. There is a third activity – caring for people's needs – which is constantly ignored. Conventional ways of looking at the economy do not distinguish between caring and consuming. And this means that when a man stays at home from work to look after his sick wife or children, that only shows up in the accounts as a *loss* of economic welfare.

People assume that what matters is the efficient organisation of production, and that greater production brings greater happiness. Of course people do need material goods. But the production of those goods relies on a system of caring which reproduces the workforce, which services it and keeps it in good working order. So production depends on *re*production. And it is wrong to think of caring or reproductive work as a drain on economic wealth. It is wrong to think that the amount we can afford to spend on it is limited by some iron law of economics, when in fact it is a political choice.

Women and the public sector

The idea that satisfying these social needs is a drain on productive resources carries over into our view of the relationship between the public and private sectors of the economy. The current British government, following to some extent from the last, has fostered the view that the public sector saps energy from the private, profit-making sector of the economy – almost like a vampire.

One reason people got this idea was because, at a time when employment in the public sector was growing, jobs were being lost in the private sector, especially in manufacturing. It was not that workers were switching jobs from manufacturing into the public services. The big change came with growth in the 1950s and 1960s, when women moved out of the household onto the labour market. Many of them went into public sector jobs. Often, these women were doing work almost identical to the unpaid work they had previously done

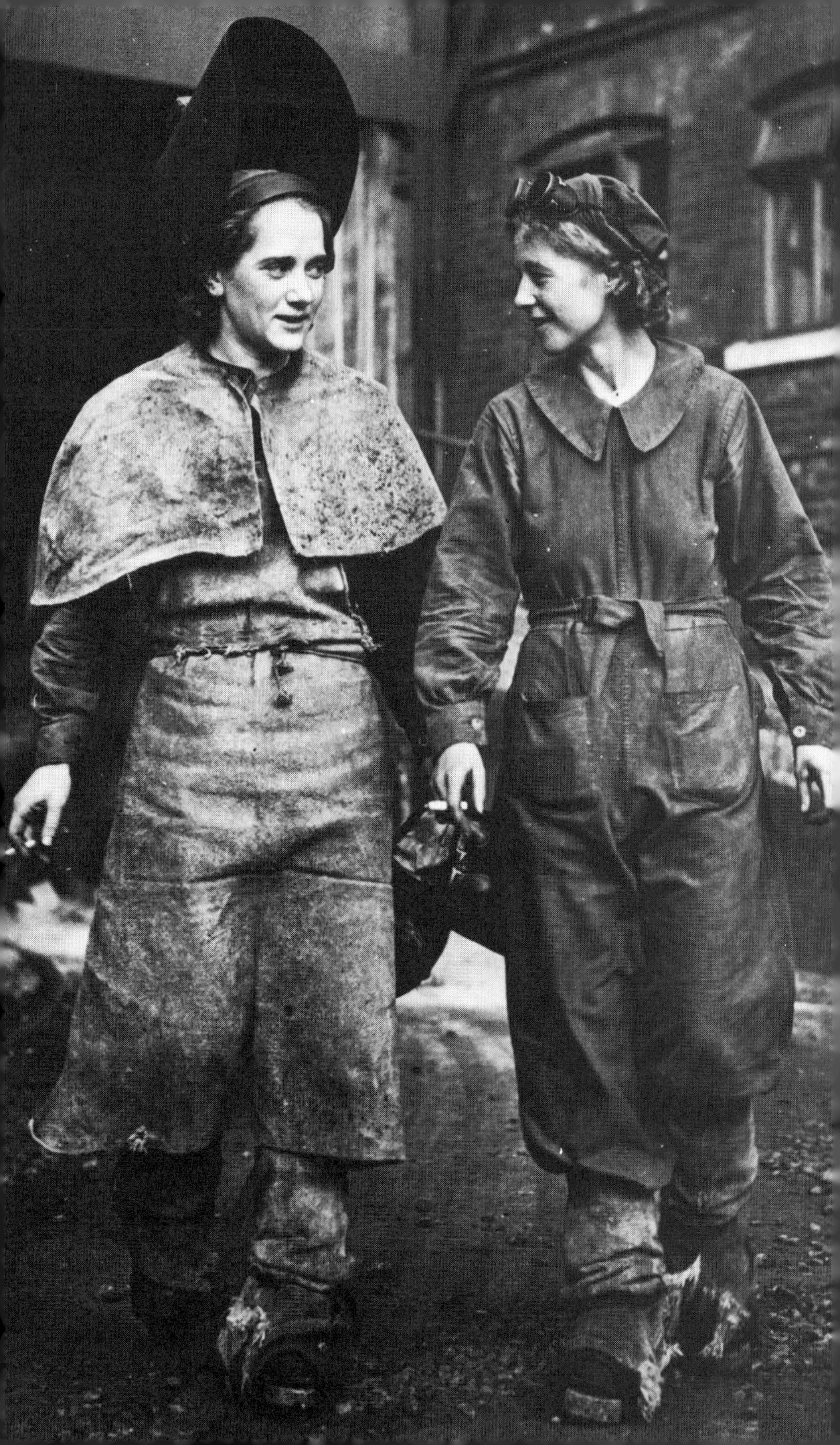

A Feminist View

in the home. But doing it as a job often made it more efficient. For example, nursery schooling expanded during this period. This meant that young children had more opportunities to learn from each other and play together, instead of being stuck at home, bored with a bored mum. And for every nursery teacher employed, some ten or twelve women were able to go out to work. Altogether about two million women came on to the labour market in this period, and without this influx economic growth would have come to a halt far sooner.

The reason why so many caring services are provided by the public sector is that they simply cannot be provided profitably by private firms. And this in turn is partly because women are still expected to do the work for free at home anyway.

So, far from being a drain on the expansion of the economy, the growth of the public sector was important in enabling women to go out to work. At the same time it was an important stimulus to economic growth.

But women were still left with the housework. This often meant they took part-time paid work close to home in a small range of jobs. Eighty per cent of women today do jobs that are 'women's work' and less than one in six are working alongside men in the same kind of work. Believe it or not, that is hardly more than were doing so at the turn of the century.

Jobs as roles

This rigid sex-casting of work may well have hampered the growth of the economy. As the Finneston Report on engineering argued, British industry has long suffered from a shortage of skilled engineers. Yet women's potential has hardly been tapped. It is not that women are constitutionally incapable of acquiring engineering skills - women showed their capability in this country during the War. But women are generally only brought in as cheap labour for jobs men do not want to do. They have been systematically excluded from large sectors of

Opposite: 'Women showed their capability ... during the War.' (Fox Photos)

the economy, such as engineering, and so have become a cheap and unskilled labour force.

As we all know, to the cost of many, the economic system is now in crisis. British capitalism, and capitalism world-wide, is in its deepest recession since the 1930s. The crisis is constantly presented as one of male employment. For a start, the official count of the unemployed ignores large numbers of women, because it only counts the registered unemployed. On this basis, the British Department of Employment figures suggest only a little more than quarter of the unemployed are women, but in reality, according to an EEC survey, nearly 40 per cent of the unemployed in Britain turn out to be women. Yet few people recognise that the problem of unemployment affects women on the same scale as men.

The headlines highlight the closure of manufacturing firms. And it is of course sad that whole areas have lost the jobs they once relied on. But the extent of the crisis tends to be measured by an inability to produce physical hardware – steel, ships, cars, etc. Economic vitality is often confused with symbols of virility. These are the sorts of jobs people think of as 'real' work, work which a nation or a man can be proud of. Manliness has become wrapped up in the heavy, dirty and dangerous work that men have been forced to do. Work in offices, hotels, shops and hospitals is somehow always second-class work. It is often treated with disdain, not only because it is less well paid, but because it is seen as women's work.

One reason for the emphasis on the loss of manufacturing jobs is what unemployment in our society does to men. Unemployment is not only a problem of poverty, but also a loss of identity, status and self-esteem. To put it another way, unemployment reduces men to the status of women, dependent and excluded.

Some unemployed men try and turn this into something positive by spending more time with their children. But the government's Manpower Services Commission keeps them on the straight and narrow.

A Feminist View

'In reality, nearly 40 per cent of the unemployed in Britain turn out to be women.' (Network)

They advise unemployed executives to 'make it clear to your family that when you are job hunting you are not on call to mend fuses, clear a blocked sink or fetch the children from school'. The rules for Unemployment and Supplementary Benefit are designed to protect men's position as heads of households and chief breadwinners even when they are unemployed. After a certain point, any money earned by the wife of an unemployed man simply leads to a cut in benefit. As a result, only one-third of the wives of unemployed men go out to work, compared to nearly two-thirds of all wives.

So the problem of unemployment is made worse by the rigid distinctions that are usually made between men's role as breadwinners and women's role as the chief care-workers in their families. But instead of trying to break down this division, one response to economic crisis is to reverse the few gains that women have made. The crude version of this calls on women to leave their jobs and get back in the home. The sophisticated version calls for public sector cuts.

Of course cutting back the public sector not only cuts women's job directly, but also makes it much more difficult for other women to go out to work. But if you try to cut women's jobs by cutting back the public sector, that does not mean manufacturing will thrive.

Women will spend less in the shops; to save money they will buy fewer convenience foods; they will make more of the family's clothes and mend old things rather than buy new things. Because they are spending less, fewer people would have jobs making things for others to buy.

Those families where women do not go out to work are three times more likely to live in poverty than those where they do. That means they are three times less likely to be able to afford a car, washing machine or a holiday. So it is very difficult to see how cutting the public sector, and with it women's employment, can restore profitability to industry.

A feminist policy for the crisis
So what should be done? A lot of people have argued, rightly, that we need massive new investment to make full use of the resources of man and woman power in our economy. But we also need the available work to be shared more fairly. A feminist response to the crisis would be to share all the available paid work. This would help to point the economy in a less male-dominated direction, as paid work and work in the home were shared more evenly between men and women.

At present, even without new investment, there are some 680 million hours of paid work available each week in the paid sector of the economy. Men do 440 million and women 240 million. With investment, particularly in labour intensive services, there could be a lot more hours work available. But even on the present basis, allowing two years' study time for all adults and time off for parents of very young children, that averages out to about 25 hours a week paid work for

Is there any need to perpetuate the usual destinction between 'male' and 'female' work? (Raisa Page)

every adult under retirement age. At first sight a 25 hour week might appear to be a cut in living standards, but it need only be a cut in men's incomes relative to women's. Total household income would be the same as before but it could be distributed more fairly.

Men work the long hours they do because they are expected to be the chief breadwinners. If women had equal access to good jobs, would there be any real need to perpetuate the division of male breadwinner and female dependant? Some might argue that reducing men's hours of work would be wasting our resources, particularly of skilled labour. But what of the massive waste of skills in today's unemployment? In any case, it is the unskilled who work the longest hours. Skills are still the privilege of the few. Women's potential to acquire skills has always been wasted in the existing division of labour.

If we did redistribute paid work in this way (say by legislating to prevent men working long hours of paid work, in the same way as legislation restricts women's hours) there need be little or no unemployment and, what is more, men, and also those without children, could share more in the work of the home and the community. Children would benefit through more contact with men (both fathers and others) and men might benefit through learning the importance of co-operative, caring work. They might even enjoy it.

Of course we cannot have a radical redistribution of paid work and household work just for the asking. There are massive vested interests in the present division of labour. The division between the household and the labour market is rooted in our capitalist economy. But that system has failed us. The economic crisis has made it clearer than ever before that the system does not provide for very basic human needs. At best, it turned men into walking wage packets, and put women in their shadow. But the best is long gone. It is about time we started thinking anew.